Praise for
Smart Business, Social Business

"*Smart Business, Social Business* is comprehensive in scope and a must-read for all businesses grappling with the rapidly changing world of social media and its potential positive (or negative) impact on business."

Chip Rodgers, Vice President and COO,
SAP Community Network, SAP AG

"Social media has empowered the social customer, which is forcing all businesses to be more human and in touch. It is imperative that companies today understand what social business means and how they can begin to effectively practice it internally and externally within their organizations. Michael Brito's book, *Smart Business, Social Business*, is an outstanding guide to understanding 'social' and the steps necessary to leverage its power to compete effectively in today's changing business landscape."

—**Jon Ferrara**, CEO, Nimble.com

"If you're not considering your customer's network value, you're a fool. Let Brito help you."

—**Joe Fernandez**, CEO and Co-founder, Klout

"Social media for enterprise markets has a much different set of complexities than social media for consumer markets. Michael Brito has successfully captured and explained these complexities in such a way that enterprise marketers can and should use this book as a how-to manual for social business for years to come."

—**Jennifer Leggio**, ZDNet business blogger and enterprise marketer

"Articulate, succinct, and inspiring! Michael has captured the essentials of running and building a business in the social media world. This is a must-read for small business owners and Fortune 500 executives alike."

—**Ted Murphy**, Founder & CEO, IZEA, Inc.

"Michael Brito is an industry veteran who's experience and knowledge shows. The guy knows the social customer. Not only does he know who it is, but he knows what businesses need to do to adjust to the new reality that the social customer brings. That can't be said about a lot of people. But once you're done reading this book, you'll know it can be said about Michael Brito."

—**Paul Greenberg**, Author, *CRM at the Speed of Light*

SMART BUSINESS,

A Playbook for Social Media in Your Organization

SOCIAL BUSINESS

MICHAEL BRITO

800 East 96th Street,
Indianapolis, Indiana 46240 USA

Smart Business, Social Business

Library of Congress Cataloging-in-Publication Data:

Brito, Michael.
  Smart business, social business : a playbook for social media in your organization / Michael Brito.
      p. cm.
  Includes index.
  ISBN 978-0-7897-4799-0
  1. Marketing—Social aspects. 2. Online social networks. 3. Internet marketing. 4. Management—Social aspects. 5. Social responsibility of business. I. Title.
  HF5415.B6735 2012
  658.8'72—dc23

                                    2011020995

Printed in the United States of America

First Printing: July 2011

Trademarks

All terms mentioned in this book that are known to be trademarks or service marks have been appropriately capitalized. Que Publishing cannot attest to the accuracy of this information. Use of a term in this book should not be regarded as affecting the validity of any trademark or service mark.

Mac is a registered trademark of Apple Corporation, Inc. Windows is a registered trademark of Microsoft Corporation

Warning and Disclaimer

Bulk Sales

Que Publishing offers excellent discounts on this book when ordered in quantity for bulk purchases or special sales. For more information, please contact

> U.S. Corporate and Government Sales
> 1-800-382-3419
> corpsales@pearsontechgroup.com

For sales outside of the U.S., please contact

> International Sales
> international@pearson.com

ISBN-13: 978-0-7897-4799-0
ISBN-10: 0-7897-4799-5

Editor-in-Chief
Greg Wiegand

Acquisitions Editor
Michelle Newcomb

Development Editor
Leslie T. O'Neill

Managing Editor
Kristy Hart

Senior Project Editor
Lori Lyons

Copy Editor
Krista Hansing Editorial Services, Inc.

Indexer
Lisa Stumpf

Proofreader
Apostrophe Editing Services

Technical Editor
Rebecca Lieb

Publishing Coordinator
Cindy Teeters

Book Designer
Anne Jones

Compositor
Nonie Ratcliff

CONTENTS AT A GLANCE

TABLE OF CONTENTS

About the Author

Michael Brito is a vice president at Edelman Digital and leads the digital team in Silicon Valley. He provides strategic counsel, guidance, and best practices to several of Edelman's top global tech accounts and is responsible for driving new business, growing existing business, mentoring junior staff members, and maintaining strong client relationships. Previously, Michael worked for major companies in Silicon Valley, including Sony Electronics, Hewlett Packard, Yahoo!, and Intel Corporation, working in various marketing, social media, and community management roles.

He is the founder of Silicon Valley Tweetup and is actively involved in the Social Media Club, Silicon Valley Chapter. He is a business advisor for the social media marketing company Izea and online resource MarketingZone.com; a business advisor to Lonesome George & Co.; and he is an early investor of social business hub OneForty. He is a frequent speaker at industry conferences as well as a guest lecturer at various universities, including Cal Berkeley, the University of San Francisco, Stanford University, Syracuse University, Golden Gate University, and Saint Mary's College of California.

Michael has a Bachelor of Arts in Business degree from Saint Mary's College and a Master of Science, Integrated Marketing Communications degree from Golden Gate University. He proudly served eight years in the United States Marine Corps.

Michael believes that marketing can be evil at times; but if done right, it can drive customer loyalty, product innovation, and brand advocacy. He believes that marketers need to spend more time listening to the social customer and less time sending one-way marketing messages. He is confident that if brands love their customers, they'll love them back and tell others about it. He also believes that organizations cannot and will not have effective, external conversations with consumers unless they can have effective internal conversations first.

Dedication

This book is dedicated to the three most important girls in my life: Kathy, Milan, and Savannah. Without your laughter, smiles, hugs, kisses, support, and sacrifice, I would be nothing. You truly give my life meaning.

Acknowledgments

First and foremost, I would like to thank God for giving me the strength and resilience it took to complete this book. I have to say that it was one of the hardest things I have ever done in my life. When my to-do list piled up higher and higher and there was no end in sight, he was the one who helped me through all the stressful times.

I also want to thank my wife Kathy for her sacrifice and support while I spent most every weekend at Starbucks writing this book. She has been my rock since the beginning. Thank you to my two little girls, Milan and Savvy, whose smiles and kisses got me through each and every day; and for their complete understanding of my absence at Family Movie Night, our family tradition of camping out downstairs and watching movies every Friday night. A big thank you to my mom for just being mom and supporting everything I do. This book is every bit as much your accomplishment as it is mine.

I want to thank Que Publishing (Pearson), specifically my acquisition editor, Michelle, for believing in me and my vision for this book; especially when other publishers weren't giving me the time of day. And thank you to my development editor, Leslie (LTO), whose feedback was valuable in helping me become a better writer.

Thank you to my team at Edelman Digital who has supported me from the beginning: Cricket, Mary, Kevin, Jenna, Karen, Sue, Shay, Paul, Jeanette, Lisa, Terry, Sarah, Rachelle, Santiago, and Adriana. It's because of their hard work, diligence, and "get the job done" attitude that I was able to focus on writing my book during the evenings and on the weekends instead of worrying about work. I can't forget Chris L. for reviewing and giving me feedback on one of the hardest chapters in the book for me on measurement.

I also want to thank several friends and mentors who have either influenced my decision to write this book, opened some doors, or just did something awesome for me during this process. Thank you all from the bottom of my heart: Brian Solis (@briansolis), Chris Brogan (@chrisbrogan), Jeremiah Owyang (@jowyang), Krystyl Baldwin (@krystyl), Laura Fitton (@pistachio), Janet Aronica (@janetaronica), Jennifer Leggio (@mediaphyter), Gabriel Carrejo (@gabrielcarrejo),

Jay Baer (@jaybaer), Maria Ogneva (@themaria), Amber Naslund (@ambercadabra), Paul Greenberg (@pgreenbe), Becky Carroll (@bcarroll7), Paul Chaney (@pchaney), Shel Israel (@shelisreal), Aaron Strout (@aaronstrout), Justin Levy (@justinlevy), Jacob Morgan (@jacobm), Mike Stelzner (@mike_stelzner), Jim Tobin (@jtobin), Robin Miller (@RobinWithAnI), Chuck Hemman (@chuckhemann), Adam Schoenfeld (@schoeny), Vilma Bonilla (@Vilma_Bonilla), Andy Smith (@kabbenbock), Adam Helweh (@secretsushi), Betsy Soler (@bsoler), Brian Remmel (@Bremmel), and so many more.

I also want to thank all my Facebook friends for their "Likes," encouragement, and for sharing my book with friends. I have a special place in my heart for all of you. And I can't thank my Twitter community enough for their consistent retweets and encouragement. I love you all.

A big thank you to everyone who helped me contribute to this book, specifically Kelly Feller and Bryan Rhoads from Intel, Len Devanna from EMC, Petra Neiger from Cisco, Rohit Bhargava from Ogilvy, Ben Parr from Mashable, Cara Fugetta from Zuberance, Maria Poveromo and Maria Yap from Adobe, David Alston from Radian6, Joe Chernov from Eloqua, and all the other vendors I featured in the book—too many to list.

Without all of your help and support, none of this would have been possible.

We Want to Hear from You!

As the reader of this book, *you* are our most important critic and commentator. We value your opinion and want to know what we're doing right, what we could do better, what areas you'd like to see us publish in, and any other words of wisdom you're willing to pass our way.

As an associate publisher for Que Publishing, I welcome your comments. You can email or write me directly to let me know what you did or didn't like about this book—as well as what we can do to make our books better.

Please note that I cannot help you with technical problems related to the topic of this book. We do have a User Services group, however, where I will forward specific technical questions related to the book.

When you write, please be sure to include this book's title and author as well as your name, email address, and phone number. I will carefully review your comments and share them with the author and editors who worked on the book.

Email: feedback@quepublishing.com

Mail: Greg Wicgand
             Editor-in-Chief
             Que Publishing
             800 East 96th Street
             Indianapolis, IN 46240 USA

Reader Services

Visit our website and register this book at quepublishing.com/register for convenient access to any updates, downloads, or errata that might be available for this book.

Foreword by Brian Solis

Adapting Businesses to Meet the Needs of the Connected Customer

The social media movement is far more important than we realize. Several years ago I compared the democratization of information to the economic impact realized during the Industrial Revolution. Indeed, social media is much more than Twitter, Facebook, and YouTube. Social media is a lens into the future of business and the relationships that are created between brands and customers. However, social media can only benefit the organization if its promise is unlocked across the entire organization and not siloed in any one department or function.

Hosting a dynamic Facebook presence and active Twitter stream does not make a business *social*. Pointing to these accounts in marketing and advertising material also do not make a business social. So what, then, defines a social business?

A social business is one with its communities, wherever they reside. As customers view businesses as one brand and not as a series of disconnected units or departments, a social business is connected, engaged, and adaptive. United on all fronts, a social business connects the dots between value and customer experiences as it heralds a new era of relationships and operates under a banner of transparency and open leadership.

Once-reluctant businesses are now increasingly turning to social media as a means of capturing customer attention. Read any blog or turn to any mainstream media source, and you'll find countless stories of how social media represent the panacea for all business ills. These ills, however, plague every business. While social media represent a wonderful opportunity for businesses to get closer to their customers, businesses could also benefit from a little soul searching. Why? In addition to improving customer relationships, social media also represent an amplifier for all aspects of customer experiences—the good, bad, and the ugly.

Despite this realization, businesses invest in the cultivation of dedicated communities in fledging social networks because there's a prevailing perception of necessity, or in some cases it's recognized as a tactical advantage. We don't have to venture too far before we stumble upon success story after success story. For example, Coca-Cola has impressively amassed 26 million "Likes" on Facebook, and the Starbucks fandom has percolated to 22 million. These examples become the standard to which other businesses aspire and serve as best practices for others to follow.

These social presences offer the semblance of consumer magnetism and honestly, the numbers are nothing short of staggering. In comparison, traffic to the traditional web sites for Coca-Cola and Starbucks pale by comparison at 270,000 and 1.8 million monthly visitors, respectively. With every example we read, we're led to believe that Facebook, Twitter, et al represent sure-fire magnets for customer attention and catalysts for interaction—and ultimately loyalty. At the same time, presences in social media enable and inevitably invite customer engagement and feedback. A social business looks at customer activity and designs click paths and experiences internally to guide external experiences.

In a 2010 study, my colleague at Altimeter Group, Jeremiah Owyang, examined the social media architectures within enterprise businesses and found that 50% of all social media initiatives reside within the marketing department. When combined with corporate communications and web/digital teams, almost 90% of social media is siloed within a marketing function and thus trapping social media's potential at transforming the organization into a social business. Thus, it's time to rethink the future of social media. If businesses are truly to become social businesses, they must match the behavior of customers to effectively meet their needs and expectations instead of simply responding to them.

Everything begins with the realization that customer needs and characteristics aren't created equally. In order for businesses to truly become social, the tenets of social media must permeate the entire organization. These businesses build a foundation based on three important pillars:

Connected

Engaged

Adaptive

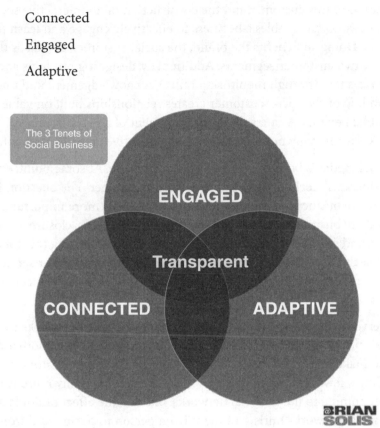

These pillars prepare a business for the dynamic nature of customer engagement across the distinct categories that define what I call a "market in transition." This shifting landscape is segmenting the customer base into three very distinct groups: traditional, online, and now social. This social customer is important because he finds and shares information, qualifies prospects, and makes decisions unlike the other two groups. As a result, they require a different level of engagement. They're connected. They're influential. Their experiences steer the actions of others. Engaging them and building a business to support them over time, is mutually beneficial.

How customers use social technology opens new feedback loops that teach those who listen…namely, the social business. It is in the identification of this customer and the construction of an interactive social framework that enables a business to effectively engage and learn from them. Doing so benefits the brand, the social customer, as well as the other two customer segments. Additionally, designing products and services that through monitoring reflect acknowledgement and understanding of the social customer creates relationships built on value and mutual benefits. As a result, the development of a social business makes a company not only modern and adaptive, but also relevant.

Social media is both a right and a rite of passage. At some point, every business will feel the power of their social customer. The question is, what are businesses going to do about it? Perhaps more importantly, what are businesses going to do with feedback to offer closure, resolution, and steer positive outcomes. It starts with connecting the dots between marketing and customer service, between customer service and product development, and also across all departments affected by, or possess the capacity to affect, outside social activity.

Everyday customers are increasingly relying on social networks as their primary way to connect and communicate with one another and also make important decisions. The old adage of happy customers telling a few friends and unhappy customers telling many more is not only coming to life in social networks, but also the effect of doing so in social networks hurls sentiment from person to person and from network to network across hundreds and even thousands with every Like, ReTweet, comment, and reaction.

Listening to the social customer is just the beginning. Responding to them when they're in need or simply to express gratitude in real time in their channels of relevance opens a door that cannot be closed. Unlike Pandora's infamous box, the resulting activities and the change in dynamics of business is not unwise—it is, to the contrary, shrewd and necessary. The door of self-expression was opened with or without your consent. For those businesses that seek engagement and relevance in new media, let's consider the broader implications of a simple conversation. In fact, think of a conversation as a conduit for desirable outcomes that carry benefits on all sides of the customer equation.

Today, getting closer to customers is a top priority for executives. It's almost ironic considering that mainstream business practices were almost in direct conflict with this new sense of renewed customer centricity. Over the years, businesses have moved in an opposite direction distancing representatives from customers through technology, automated process, and through the introduction of outsourced representatives. Customers were practically penalized for trying to seek attention. All was done, however, in the name of operationalization, efficiency, and profitability.

Now we see an about-face through the convergence of media, marketing, and service. Businesses now aspire to social prominence following in the digital footsteps of the much publicized and studied examples of @ComcastCares and @ATT on Twitter. In these cases, if a customer Tweets a problem or a question, Comcast and AT&T have fully staffed Twitter and other social media accounts ready to listen and also respond when necessary. Empowerment is an important characteristic for a social business. Often these representatives can solve problems on the spot or retrieve useful information or trigger next steps to achieve resolution. But at the same time, the shared experiences of customers also vocalize recurring trends that require that attention of other departments. Before we can collaborate externally, we must first collaborate within. Doing so creates processes and systems that proactively fix problems through constant product improvement, redesign, or further experimentation. Most representatives on social networks are disconnected from influencing or expediting internal change for the betterment of the customer experience and ultimately the sentiment associated with the brand. A social business is designed to optimize experiences.

Whether it's through traditional means or through social networks, responding to problems is by default reactive and focused solely on negative origins. Although still important and necessary, reactive-based engagement attempts to change customer perceptions or impressions once they're already experienced. Proactively translating that insight into continuous innovation positions the businesses toward a much more productive position, one where positive experiences eclipse the unfavorable.

A good business will use social networks to identify and solve problems as they arise. A social business will then connect the dots within the organization to adapt and positively steer experiences of connected customers through an integrated approach—an approach of oneness. A social business will design the organizational framework to liberate social media from any one department and focus while uniting silos to connect, engage, and adapt. As a result, success will then be measured in sentiment, referrals, and loyalty.

Whether in social networks or in real life, people naturally share experiences. In the end, customers will inevitably share experiences whether they're negative or positive. The opportunity here is that now more than ever, businesses have a say in the matter. They can choose whether those shared experiences are positive or negative, starting at the development of a product or service and enlivened through the company's sales, marketing, and service programs. The social customer for all intents and purposes deserves a seat on the board of advisors of any social business. They are stakeholders. They are the guiding light toward relevance and success. And, they require nothing less than the complete transformation of business.

I've had the opportunity to work with Michael Brito over the years, and his work is nothing short of inspirational. In this book, Michael shares his insights into the needs of a new generation of connected customers and the importance of building an adaptive framework of a social business. In Smart Business, Social Business Brito gives you actionable steps to help you chart your course toward success. By the time you're done reading this book you will not only get closer to customers, but learn how to place customers at the front-and-center of all aspects of business where social equates to relevance and where relevance equals allegiance.

You are the architects of a new era of business where adaptive organizations are measured by the ability to shape and steer positive customer experiences before, during, and after transactions.

Brian Solis
Principal of Altimeter Group and
Author of *Engage!* and *The End of Business as Usual*

Introduction

This is not a book about social media marketing. Within these pages, you'll find no hidden formula that will teach a business how to increase friends, fans, and followers. It's not a book about viral marketing, and it doesn't condone using social media to broadcast one-way messages to the masses. This book is different.

Many organizations today spend a lot of time, resources, and money trying to understand the social landscape and engaging externally with their customers and prospects. They're on a quest to become a social brand. They're investing in Facebook applications, branded communities, and blogs; many also are using online monitoring solutions to listen and see what people are saying about the brand. From this perspective, many companies today are doing a decent job.

Friends, fans, and followers are important, yes. And brands increase their social equity by engaging in two-way dialogue with their constituency, yes. And transparency is key to these external engagements, yes. But while many organizations are trying desperately to humanize their brand, they are failing to understand that they need to humanize their business first.

Therein lies the business challenge. As social network sites such as Facebook and Twitter gained popularity and social customers became more influential, companies of all sizes and from all industries began to join the conversation. Customers learned to expect companies to be part of the social web. And social influencers started criticizing brands for every action—or inaction—they took online.

Companies listened. Organizations are now aggressively hiring community managers and social strategists, allocating budgets to social media, hiring agencies, and creating engagement strategies. They are doing everything a "good" social brand should be doing.

But this book is not about social brands. It's about an organization's natural (sometimes forced) evolution into a social business. A social business deals with the internal transformation of an organization and addresses key factors such as organizational models, culture, internal communications, collaboration, governance, training, employee activation, global and technology expansion, team dynamics, and measurement philosophy.

To do this effectively, companies have to get smarter; acquire new technologies, intelligence, and talent; and become more open and transparent. They have to establish business processes, governance models and rules of engaging on the social web that protect the organization yet empower their employees. They have to change the way they do business—and that starts with the people of the organization.

An organization that uses social media to engage externally with customers is a social brand but not necessarily a social business. There's a huge difference between the two.

From the outside looking in, most people wouldn't recognize or understand the challenges that social media has created in an enterprise. The anarchy, conflict, confusion, lack of communication and collaboration, and organizational silos that exist behind the firewall are not visible. These challenges make the process of becoming an effective social brand much more difficult and less effective. For some organizations, this quest to become a social brand and a social business is done simultaneously.

The premise of this book is that organizations cannot and will not have effective external conversations with consumers unless they can have effective internal conversations first. This involves much more than internal conversations, conference calls, and a collaboration forum. For this evolution to take place, organizations need to adopt social behaviors in every aspect of their business.

Figure I.1 illustrates the evolution of social business. It started with the growing influence of the social customer. The immediate response to the social customer was that companies began to adopt behaviors of a social brand—brands/companies and organizations started engaging with the social customer on the social web. Today, this is causing a multitude of challenges internally, such as no governance and policies, employees running wild in social media, social media ownership issues, and more for many organizations. Now organizations are trying to operationalize social media internally to become a collaborative social business.

THE EVOLUTION OF SOCIAL BUSINESS		2008 to Present
		SOCIAL BUSINESS
	2003 to Present	
	SOCIAL BRAND	
1995 to Present		
SOCIAL CUSTOMER		
• Technology Innovation gives customers a voice • They are Influential • Amplified voice across the social web • Google indexing critical conversations about companies • Social Customers are trusted among their peers as influence grows	• Companies and brands join Twitter, Facebook, and create corporate blogs • Engage with the social customer in various channels • Social Media teams are forming slowly • Small budgets are allocated on a project basis to social media engagement and community building	• Organizations begin humanizing business operations • Organizational models are formed to include social media • Organizational silos are torn down between internal teams • Governance models and social media policies are created • Social becomes an essential attribute of organizational culture

Figure I.1 *The evolution of social business*

This is the key takeaway of this book.

This book aims to equip business leaders, marketers, and communications professionals with the knowledge necessary to transform their business. It provides actionable insights for them to take back to their teams and organizations to begin facilitating change. The social business evolution will not happen overnight. It may take years. But it has to happen and it will happen. This book helps make that happen.

Chapters at a Glance

Chapter 1, "Human Capital, Evolved," deals with the organization's most valuable asset: its people. It addresses the need to facilitate organizational change in an effort to break down organizational silos and communicate more effectively. Much of that communication should involve organizational failures in the social space so that teams can learn what not to do and avoid making the same mistake more than once. The chapter also discusses the importance of gaining executive support from either the CEO or someone close to him or her who can champion the evolution internally. A big part of this chapter discusses the need to empower employees to engage in the social web; it offers examples of how to manage teams and employees across different business units and geographies. The chapter concludes with an overview of three common organizational models related to social media: centralized, decentralized, and a fully collaborative and integrated social model.

Chapter 2, "Surveying The Technology Supermarket," discusses technology and the importance of choosing the right social software. It's not a comprehensive overview of every technology vendor in the market; rather, it covers a subset of vendors—some old, some new—that are driving innovation on the social web. The chapter discusses collaboration/internal community software, social listening, and social relationship management vendors. It also discusses the importance of internal scalability and the need to have IT involved when sourcing vendors. The chapter concludes by making a few predictions on the social landscape for Facebook and Twitter.

Chapter 3, "Establishing a Governance Model," discusses the need for organizations to establish governance models that address employees' use of social media, disclosure, and moderation policies (on and off domain). Several real-life (and very public) examples illustrate what happens when organizations do not have policies in place to guide employee behavior. The chapter also discusses the need for organizations to become more intelligent through ongoing training opportunities and through noncompetitive collaboration with other companies to share enterprise best practices. The chapter concludes with a discussion of the need to create social media executive councils that will help shape governance, training, and deployment internally.

Chapter 4, "Embracing the Social Consumer," discusses the evolution of social customers and their growing influence on the social web. It also covers their business counterpart: the social media practitioner, the employee responsible for establishing, fostering, and guiding a conversational exchange with the social customer. The chapter also discusses the difference between corporate social profiles and personal profiles as this relates to social media practitioners. Much of this chapter also illustrates the importance of integrating customer support into social media, as well as using the channels to solicit feedback from the community.

Chapter 5, "In Response to the Social Customer: Social CRM," is all about social CRM. It defines the process of managing and responding to the social customer via social CRM channels. The chapter goes in depth about various applications and use case models of social CRM and categorizes different types of customers that organizations must pay attention to. Roles and responsibilities are also discussed. The chapter concludes by highlighting three vendors that are taking social CRM to the next level.

Chapter 6, "Establishing a Measurement Philosophy," discusses the importance for organizations to agree on a measurement philosophy that works for everyone. The chapter also discusses financial impact and nonfinancial impact-measurement philosophies, including ROI-driven metrics, purchase funnel metrics, owned-earned-paid media values, community health, and share of voice metrics. The chapter concludes with a discussion of how to measure influence, the value of a Facebook fan, and challenges that organizations will face when determining a measurement philosophy.

Chapter 7, "How to Choose the Right Vendors, Agencies, and Technology Partners," outlines a step-by-step process for choosing the right technology vendors and spotlights issues to consider before making any purchase decisions. Additionally, the chapter highlights three agency perspectives and three perspectives from Fortune 500 companies (Intel, Cisco, and Adobe) and shares valuable advice on what to consider when selecting a social agency. It concludes with a quick case study showcasing Cisco and its process for choosing technology vendors.

Chapter 8, "Marketing Investments on the Rise for Social Business Initiatives," discusses the recent trend of organizations allocating marketing dollars to social business budgets, both internally and externally. The chapter cites several research studies from eMarketer, MarketingSherpa, Econsultancy, ExactTarget, Meltwater, StrongMail, Zoomerang, and Alterian as it relates to 2011 predictions and insights into social media budgets within the organization. The chapter also highlights data from the Altimeter Group as to which job functions and social media initiatives the budget dollars are getting allocated to. The chapter concludes with a framework that organizations can use to determine budgets internally and to develop buy-in and support from senior management.

Chapter 9, "Creating a Comprehensive Social Media Strategic Plan," helps business leaders and marketers define and create a comprehensive social media strategy, taking into consideration the difference in an organization's mission, goals and objectives, strategy, and tactical plans. The chapter goes in depth to explain the value of audience segmentation and gives global snapshots of social media usage, behaviors, and adoption in Latin America, Europe, and Asia Pacific. Finally, it discusses the importance of integrating social media with paid media.

Chapter 10, "The Rise of Customer Advocacy," examines the difference between influencers and advocates. The chapter details how to create a robust customer advocacy program and highlights a well-known vendor's program. The chapter concludes with a case study about marketing automation SaaS company Eloqua.

Chapter 11, "Ethical Bribe: Relevant Content Matters," is about content. It discusses how strategic, relevant content can add business value to the online conversation. The chapter gives specific recommendations for companies on adding value to the conversation, becoming a trusted advisor, being authentic and believable, building trust, and listening. Relevant content can increase the reach of branded messages and increase the organic search results for certain terms.

Chapter 12, "Social Businesses in the Real World: EMC and Intel," highlights two case studies of companies that exemplify the characteristics of a social business and are succeeding in the social space, EMC and Intel. EMC first gained focus internally and created a fully collaborative, social organization before unleashing its employees externally to engage with customers. Intel, on the other hand, began its journey as a grassroots effort more than 10 years ago when technology experts and IT managers were engaging in forums and chat rooms, talking shop with other IT managers. This natural groundswell effect from employees, coupled with management's vision to socialize the organization, drove Intel to become a leading brand in social media.

Based on Actual Events

The views, theories, strategies, and recommendations presented in this book are the culmination of my 12 years of experience working in the enterprise; I've held positions in top technology firms such as Sony Electronics, Hewlett-Packard, Yahoo!, and Intel Corporation and have specialized in building social media programs that focus on building long-term relationships with customers. In short, I consider myself not an academic, but rather a practitioner with practical in-the-trenches experience and real-world perspectives.

That said, it's important to make a distinction between this book and many others written on the topic of social media. Most of them are written specifically from the theoretical perspective, which makes sense because of the relative newness of social media, especially within business. Here, however, I've focused on practical strategies, tactics, and lessons learned, which can effectively evolve internal culture into something that is much more appropriate and effective for today's social business.

Hopefully you'll find such an approach a refreshing change that allows you to quickly and easily apply the ideas presented to your business.

1

Human Capital, Evolved

A CEO doesn't wake up one morning with the realization that he needs to transform his organization and evolve into a social business. He has more important things to worry about, like increasing market share, revenues, shareholders, and board meetings. The transformation into a social business happens organically—often in silos—and in response to the social customer.

The social customer is nothing new. Since the beginning of modern business, consumers have been sharing their thoughts, opinions, joys, fears, and criticisms with their friends, family, community groups, and even strangers about the brands they love and the ones they hate. The difference today is that these opinions are now amplified on the social web and also making their way into the search engine results.

The social customer is forcing business to operationalize social media internally in an effort to be more human externally. A social business deals with the internal transformation of an organization and addresses key factors such as organizational models, culture, internal communications, governance, training, employee activation, global and technology expansion, team dynamics, and establishing a measurement philosophy.

> The transformation into a social business happens organically—often in silos—and in response to the social customer.

First and foremost, an organization must focus on the internal fabric that makes up its business DNA—culture.

Driving Cultural Change in the Social Business

The evolution of a social business requires a paradigm shift. Employees at every level, starting at the very top, need to change their thinking, embrace new technologies, and shift their focus from sending marketing messages to building relationships. A social business is one that is open and transparent, communicates internally with stakeholders, and looks beyond organizational silos. A social business uses and adopts new tools and technologies to communicate with customers more effectively. It even changes business models, products, and processes based on collective intelligence of community feedback.

A social business forces cultural change. This happens when a company truly cares about the community and wants to meet the demands of the social customer. Why? Because social customers are voicing their opinions online on Facebook, Twitter, Amazon, and many other channels about the products they buy and use every day. These customers are influential and, in some cases, have large audiences.

Many times, cultural change is based on a "push" model. Business leaders want to change the organization (process, internal structures, behaviors, culture, values, and so on) and expect employees to follow

suit. Resistance to this type of change is normal. Employees undoubtedly will rush to defend the status quo if they feel their security, job
status, or function is threatened. This naturally creates cynicism and
resistance and, in some cases, makes it difficult for senior management
to move an organization forward in any capacity, much less fully
evolve into a social business.

Companies that are using Enterprise 2.0 technologies (collaboration
tools such as Yammer, Hearsay Social, and internal social networks
powered by applications such as Lithium) are more likely to be open
to a "pull" approach to cultural change. Change initiatives come from
the top down and meet in the middle from a bottom-up approach.
The great news is that these social tools are already becoming a driving force to change. The challenge arises in certain organizations when
employees don't know how to use these tools or, worse, are prohibited
from using them because they're against company policy.

The drive to become a social business requires a cultural shift that
starts at the core of the organization, with the leaders who represent
the brand. If the entire organization can be convinced that a smart
business is a social business that builds processes, infrastructures, and
programs with the customer in mind, it will begin to see positive
change both internally and externally.

Figure 1.1 illustrates that people, process, and technology are the
essential DNA to facilitate the evolution of a social business.

A social business deals with the internal dynamics of an organization
that can be grouped in three different categories. The first category
deals with the company's most valuable asset, the human capital of the
organization. It addresses the need to drive organizational change in
an effort to break down organizational silos and get internal teams to
communicate. It also involves the importance of achieving executive
support; either the CEO or someone close to him or her who will
champion social media adoption from the top down.

The second category deals with process. This simply means that
organizations need to put processes and frameworks in place to manage the chaos that exists from behind the firewall. Training, social
media guidelines, moderation policies, and global expansion must be

wrapped in various governance models that ensure message consistency, protects the organization, and also empowers its employees.

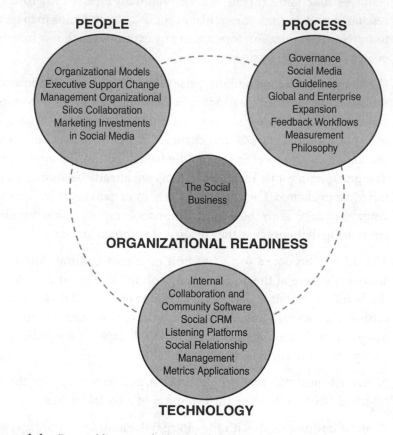

PEOPLE

Organizational Models
Executive Support Change
Management Organizational
Silos Collaboration
Marketing Investments
in Social Media

PROCESS

Governance
Social Media
Guidelines
Global and Enterprise
Expansion
Feedback Workflows
Measurement
Philosophy

The Social
Business

ORGANIZATIONAL READINESS

Internal
Collaboration and
Community Software
Social CRM
Listening Platforms
Social Relationship
Management
Metrics Applications

TECHNOLOGY

Figure 1.1 *A social business deals with the internal dynamics of every organization.*

The third category deals with technology. Organizations have to invest in platforms that facilitate internal collaboration, community building, social listening, measurement, and social relationship management. Social CRM also plays a significant role within this pillar. The challenge is that there are so many technology platforms to choose from. Organizations need to think strategically before making the investment to ensure the technology can scale and integrate with applications that already exist in the enterprise.

Tearing Down the Silos for Organizational Growth

One of the biggest challenges of cultural change is tearing down organizational silos. An organizational silo occurs when employees within various departments or business units work in a vacuum without considering the impact of their actions or inactions on the entire organization.

The end result is lack of communication and integration, displaced goals, and no clear vision. Naturally, this creates customer confusion and conflict between departments. For example, in many companies, marketing and PR teams rarely communicate with each other. And the irony of social media is that both of these job functions may require the use of external tools such as Twitter to engage with customers. If these two teams aren't talking internally or aren't integrated, they will confuse customers with multiple marketing messages. This is a common scenario in business today. Conflict and chaos arise when there's no clear definition of the goals and no plan for who is actually responsible for social media.

Many companies today are not only incapable of communicating internally with each other, but they're also unwilling and often refuse to share knowledge. It's a form of job protection, ego, or simply ignorance because people normally resist change. It's uncomfortable.

Yahoo! is one example of a company that operates in silos. Perhaps this is one reason why Yahoo! has been struggling over the last few years to regain relevance and search share, launch new products, and innovate with the social web. Each product group (Mail, Answers, Search, the Home Page, Groups, OMG, and so on) is its own self-sustaining business with isolated marketing and PR teams, finance, product management, and engineering. Rarely, if ever, do they collaborate or launch integrated campaigns in the market place. Even worse, most employees often hear news about product launches, corporate campaigns, and even layoffs from third-party sources such as Techcrunch. So it's not just about silos but poor communication from senior management.

Of course, people aren't always the ones responsible for creating silos. Isolated systems and old technologies, dated applications, and 20-year-old processes exist that keep valuable information, workflows, and transactions from moving freely and efficiently throughout an organization. Companies originally created silos to accomplish various tasks: sell products, provide customer support, advertise their products, and so on. The lack of knowledge sharing exists because there's no governance or guidance on how these functions can work together to increase efficiencies, save money, and, more importantly, provide a more positive customer experience.

Now with the rise of social customers, who have no problem expressing their opinions online, it's even more important for internal teams to communicate—not just to share knowledge and have a conversation, but to meet and exceed customer expectations. This is the core reason companies need to move from being merely a business that sometimes engages in social media to being a *real* social business.

Data confirms that consumers want to have ongoing conversations with brands. According to a study by Cone in 2009, 78 percent of consumers use social media to interact with companies in different ways, up 20 points from 2008. Unfortunately, some companies are not doing a very good job at it, especially the ones that operate in a vacuum.

For example, based on the above data and common knowledge in the space, there is a conversation happening between a brand and its customers. And as in most relationships, conversations need to evolve, grow, and add value. The last thing customers want to do is have a fragmented conversation with a company in which they must constantly reiterate their needs on social channels such as Facebook, Twitter, a company blog, and a toll-free customer service line. Different groups then end up telling the customer the same thing over and over again (usually because internal teams don't collaborate), and the problem never gets solved. The end result is a very unhappy customer who usually tells others about her experience.

Silos create equally dangerous internal situations. In many large organizations, the corporate communications team is responsible for monitoring external conversations. Many of these conversations are related to customer support and products, and much of the feedback from customers never gets sent to the appropriate teams. How can a support department address customer issues—or, better yet, change processes to actually fix the problem—if it doesn't know these conversations even took place? Just as important, how can a product organization use the collective intelligence of the community to innovate products if employees aren't privy to these valuable conversations?

Plenty of upset customers have posted on blogs, Twitter, and Facebook about experiences dialing into customer service only to be told that there's no record of their account or purchase information and then transferred from extension to extension without resolution. Unfortunately, this is a common scenario that leaves many executives shaking their head and shrugging their shoulders in amazement that they're unable to satisfy their most important asset: the customer.

By tearing down silos that prevent communication, organizations can solve a multitude of challenges, including these:

- Customer frustration
- Customer retention
- Inconsistent marketing messages
- Multiple contests or marketing campaigns that address the same customer at the same time
- Multiple branded or unbranded Facebook fan pages and Twitter profiles
- Cost inefficiencies due to duplicated effort
- Multiple contracts signed with the same vendor
- Inability to scale programs because of a lack of integration and resources

Tearing down organizational silos isn't easy to do. It requires a firm commitment from senior-level management across all business units (marketing, public relations, operations, engineering, information technology, human resources, and privacy) and a cultural transformation that empowers employees of all levels to do what's already a significant part of their DNA: be social and communicate!

Part of an effective internal communications strategy is to be open, honest, and transparent about mistakes made in social media. This is the only way an organization can grow, learn, and adjust their external communication programs.

Communicating Successful Failures

Companies need to get smarter. If they want to integrate social into every fabric of their business, they need to work through the silos, change their culture, and start communicating with each other, even if it means admitting that they screwed up along the way. From a pure social media perspective, successful failure at many large enterprises involves removing the fear of failure and replacing it with genuine encouragement to try new things, fail intelligently, and learn from mistakes.

Failing gracefully can bring about these benefits:

- Mitigated risk of duplicated failures
- Reduced anxiety
- Improved communication
- A more open intra-/cross-departmental dialogue
- More calculated risk taking in the future

Also keep in mind that failure, which *will* happen sooner or later, offers a unique opportunity to display the corporate character behind the firewall. For example, in early November 2010, rumors quickly spread across Twitter that a Qantas Airlines jet airliner had crashed on Batam Island in Indonesia.

Qantas Airlines: No Crash, Despite Lots of Rumors

After an emergency landing, rumors of a Qantas Airlines plane crash circulated unchecked. Tweets such as these left little reason to doubt what was being said:

@oneclammy: Plane crash off Indonesia, speculation that it could have been a Qantas jet headed for Singapore

@smillavtr: According to early reports from TV and Twitter it's a Qantas airliner which crash at Batam

@3Newseditor: Reports that a Qantas plane may be involved in a crash in Indonesia http://ow.ly/349sJ. Images of the nonexistent crash also showed up on social sharing sites, with one Tweet reading:

@erincopp: Not liking photos of the QANTAS plane crash. Way to fuel my fear of flying

Despite the rumors, no such crash had happened. A Qantas Airbus A380 had experienced engine trouble and subsequently made an emergency landing in Singapore. The Qantas Twitter accounts remained largely silent, and PR teams issued no statement or release addressing the rumor. Qantas was obviously either unaware of what was going on or unable to act on it because of a lack of a crisis communication plan, escalation protocol, or both.

Obviously, either Qantas has a problem with its crisis communication process or it doesn't take Twitter seriously enough to calm the public. The company eventually issued a statement about 12 hours after the first tweet, but that's not fast enough in today's real-time environment.

The question remains: Did Qantas learn from this communication failure? Is the company now listening to the social web and addressing small issues before they get blown out of proportion? Does it have a crisis communication plan in place in case this happens again? If it does, then this is an example of a successful failure because it forced the organization to change.

Generally speaking, most people are willing to forgive if they perceive understanding, transparency, and even repentance in a company. And often these mistakes serve a platform for changing brand perception, as with the case of Domino's Pizza.

Domino's Pizza YouTube Crisis

In April 2009, two Domino's Pizza employees filmed themselves doing disgusting things to a pizza before serving it to a customer. Then they posted the clip on YouTube as a prank for the world to watch. In just two short days, the world did watch—and that video had more than a million views. The conversation created a groundswell of anger on Twitter.

This was a major crisis for the Domino's brand, and the prank severely damaged the company's reputation. According to a study from research firm YouGov, the perception of Domino's food quality went from positive to negative almost overnight.

Domino's didn't respond for almost a week. Patrick Doyle, president of Dominos, USA, issued a sincere apology on YouTube and explained that the two employees in question had been fired and charged with a felony. Even more interesting, the prank caused Domino's to change their business model. According to Doyle's video, Domino's is now reexamining all its hiring processes to ensure that the company is hiring quality candidates. Domino's is also bringing in auditors more regularly to ensure that each franchise is as clean as humanly possible and that the food maintains high quality standards.

A few short months after this incident, Domino's began to address many complaints about the quality of the food and openly admitted to millions that it had failed to deliver on its core value proposition: a quality pizza. In December 2009, Domino's announced that it had changed its core recipe. And the buzz on the Internet is that it's pretty darn good.

It's safe to assume that Domino's is an expert on communicating successful failures because it listened to the social customer, communicated those concerns internally, and then changed its business.

Motrin: Does Anyone Listen to Baby-Wearing Moms?

With a slick new ad campaign by Motrin targeting baby-toting mothers ready for launch in November 2008, the folks at Johnson & Johnson probably couldn't have imagined the amount of free press they would soon get. Unfortunately, it was all negative. Despite efforts to reach out to moms and literally "feel their back pain," Motrin put its foot in its mouth with the new ad (see Figure 1.2).

Shortly after launching the ad on a Friday, an outcry of anger against the brand arose on Twitter and YouTube. Somehow the campaign design had failed to consider message sensitivity; the video seemed to deliver a back-handed criticism of mothers who carry babies in backpacks and Baby Bjorn–style carriers. A quick search on YouTube for

"Motrin Moms" reveals several videos posted by angry moms expressing their feelings about the ad.

Figure 1.2   *Motrin had no idea that its ad campaign had inadvertently offended many customers.*

To make matters worse, Motrin's apology took about a week to deliver and appeared unauthentic and meaningless. The brand simply posted a page with a few paragraphs on its Web site. Nonetheless, the video was taken down and the online outrage eventually died down.

It's easy to criticize Motrin for not having a crisis plan of action or for not monitoring Twitter for mentions of the brand. Many companies still struggle with this. However, when Motrin did find out about the online groundswell, the brand probably should have taken that opportunity to not only apologize to the community, but also attempt to get to know the moms it was trying to market its products to.

Listening to the social web isn't hard to do. Marketers can use a variety of listening tools to get a pulse of the conversation. What's hard is creating a plan or workflow so that when a crisis does happen, teams are ready to respond quickly, efficiently, and authentically to the social customer.

A referenced example of learning from the concept of successful failures is The Global Social Media Marketing Group within Silicon Valley networking company Cisco. This organization operates as a global social resource to Cisco and hosts a monthly Social Media Roundtable discussing, among other topics, recent successes and failures. Any failures and the learnings taken from them are examined, discussed, and shared in a nonthreatening environment that truly values the newfound understandings. The end result is a more intelligent organization.

Gaining Executive Sponsorship to Facilitate Change

As an organization changes and evolves—and topples its silos—it's important for someone at the top to be championing this effort. Embracing social media internally involves more than simply saying "We want to join the conversation" and then investing a couple hundred thousand dollars on a Facebook application promoting the next product. It's a cultural shift that starts at the core of the organization, with the leaders who represent the brand.

The most effective way to do this—and to get everyone behind social media—is to have one or more employees lead the way. It can be a midlevel manager, the CEO of a company, or someone close to the CEO's office. As an internal spokesperson, this person needs to be passionate about customers and must believe in the prospect of an integrated social media plan that spans all business units and marketing channels. He or she needs to speak with authority and serve as the change agent for the company.

Ultimately, getting an executive to sponsor social media efforts both internally and externally can have a bigger impact than choosing a lesser-known individual. An executive's built-in credibility and authority helps gain buy-in and support for new programs, culture change, collaboration, and often times budget. Even more important, this person can communicate program successes and failures to other business leaders, which might be otherwise impossible due to resource availability.

Gaining executive sponsorship sometimes happens organically. In many cases, business leaders are already personally engaged in social media and don't need to be convinced that the company needs to shift its strategy to meet the demands of the social customer. Other times, front-line managers who are actually executing programs need to persuade, convince, and sometime coerce upper management to start thinking differently. They need to be equipped with case studies, program successes, quantitative and qualitative metrics, and return on investment (ROI) projections to actually build a case. A series of small wins might even be needed to fully convince management to make more of an investment in social media.

For example, the Cisco Global Social Media Marketing group was able to find an executive sponsor named Carlos Dominguez who believes in the value of social media for building long-lasting relationships with customers. Dominguez reports to the office of the CEO and is often face-to-face with John Chambers, the Cisco president and CEO. He attends many events with high-level exposure both internally to the company and externally to the industry. He uses Twitter and blogs, and one of the favorite things listed on his biography on Cisco.com is "social media."

Dominguez is one reason Cisco is transforming the business-to-business (B2B) landscape with social media. He's a willing evangelist and is passionate about changing Cisco from the inside out so that the company can communicate more effectively externally.

Activating Employees to Engage in Social Media

When management is committed to investing in social media and the company has an evangelist spreading the gospel of social greatness, it's time to activate employees to engage externally with customers.

Every year, Edelman conducts its annual Trust Barometer, a survey that measures the level of trust that informed publics have in non-government organizations (NGOs), business, government, and media (see Figure 1.3). Not surprisingly. at the bottom of the list is advertising and corporate marketing. Individuals don't trust marketing messages. At the top of the list, the most trusted resources are industry analysts and articles in business publications. What's interesting, ranking at number three, was conversations with employees. Yes, individuals have a high degree of trust in employees of companies.

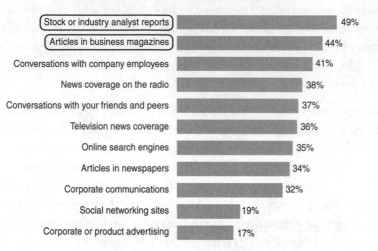

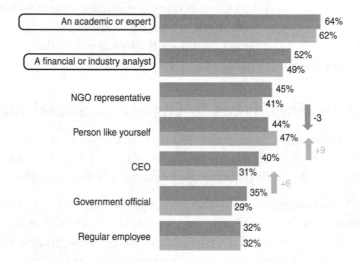

Figure 1.3 *According to the 2010 Edelman Trust Barometer, consumers put a surprising amount of trust and credibility in employees of companies (www.edelman.com/trust).*

It's important to realize that humans relate to other humans. It's ingrained in the core of personal relationships. Not often can a brand truly build strong customer relationships without some level of humanity. And humanity means having real employees interacting with real customers.

A study facilitated by Cone Research, titled *2008 Cone Business in Social Media Study* (www.coneinc.com/content1182), showed that 55 percent of consumers want ongoing conversations with companies and brands. The study investigated how brands and consumers interact and how consumers want brands to engage with them. The results were astounding. In addition to the 55 percent who wanted an ongoing interaction, 89 percent of respondents said they would feel more loyal to a brand if they were invited to take part in a feedback group.

A year later, this number went up almost 30 points. A 2009 study titled *2009 Consumer New Media Study* (www.coneinc.com/content2601) found that 85 percent of Americans who use social media think companies should have an active presence in the social media universe. Even more interesting is that those users actually want interaction with these brands. Not yet convinced? These additional data points clearly illustrate what consumers want from a brand:

Out of the 85 percent of people who want companies to be present in social media:

- 34 percent want companies to actively interact with them.

- 51 percent want companies to interact with them as needed or by request.

- 8 percent think companies should be only passively involved in social media.

- 7 percent think companies shouldn't be involved at all.

The data is clear. Consumers want to have conversations with companies they care about. They don't want to engage with corporate entities or logos, either—they want real, live human interaction and two-way dialogue with employees. And this can only be achieved with another person.

Fundamentals of Community Management

One way in which companies are activating their employees is through community managers. A community manager should be an employee of a company; in most companies, this person usually manages an editorial calendar for a blog/community, a Twitter account, and various third-party social media channels such as a Facebook fan page or a YouTube account. The best community managers usually come from the product or customer support organizations because they either know the product well or know how to resolve conflict well. Community managers play an important role because they are on the front lines of communication.

Community managers might also be responsible for managing a social listening platform such as Radian6 and for filtering/assigning conversations to others in the business unit for a proper response. They may even organize in-person events (or town halls) to get feedback from the community. Community managers are the face of the brand within social media, and conversations are at the core of their job.

Consider these top three best practices when managing a social business community:

1. **Embed within the community.**

   Community managers must embed themselves within the community they serve and become integrated within the community.
   The result is valuable data and insights collected from community members and reported back to management. This usually includes feedback on how to improve the company's products, services, or business processes.

   Community managers will succeed if they are authentic and leave their egos at the door. Community members are smart and can see right through egos—and many times they'll voice their opinions publicly if they are marketed to.

2. **Focus on community building first, monetizing second.**

   The biggest mistake a community manager can make is to start screaming one-way marketing messages at the rest of the community. The members will do one of two things: either leave the community or criticize the company publicly.

Unfortunately, situations like this do happen. Brands and small businesses create groups, fan pages, or communities for the sole reason of making money. Some sales might result, but these groups will find little to no long-term benefit, much less repeat sales. Remember the old saying, "It takes more to acquire a new customer than to sell to an existing one."

The most effective strategy to drive revenue for a business is to build the community, earn their trust, and delicately ask for permission to communicate marketing messages—wise advice from entrepreneur, author, and marketing genius Seth Godin.

Twitter is a great example of a growing company that spent almost four years just building its community and improving its product. Not once did Twitter introduce new functionality or services with the sole intent of making money. Not until early in 2010 did the company begin introducing new programs for advertisers in the form of Promoted Tweets and Promoted Trends.

3. **Don't just listen—act.**

Yes, the hot topic today is listening, and tools for that are commoditized with new applications that launch about every month. Building strong customer loyalty isn't just about listening, though—it's also about acting upon community feedback. The challenge for every business in social media is to eventually "become believable." And that means winning consumer trust.

Smart businesses aren't only listening to their customers, they're innovating and changing their products and services as a result of their feedback. For example, in late 2009, eBay (an Edelman client) launched PayPal Student Accounts, which stemmed from continued frustrations among customers who wanted family accounts. Also in 2009, Intel simply gave away T-shirts to a community that was begging for them. Starbucks (another Edelman client), one of the pioneers of this, not only solved a serious business problem of coffee spillage, but also changed the customer experience for millions by creating the

Starbucks Splash Stick in 2008 which prevents coffee from spilling out of their lids. This started as an idea posted by a customer at the My Starbucks Idea site.

These three brands share more in common than just the fact that they're listening to their customers. They were also cited in a recent study by Altimeter Group in conjunction with Wetpaint titled *Deep Brand Engagement Correlates with Financial Performance*. The report examined the top 50 brands and measured their depth of engagement with consumers on the Web; then it looked at their financial performance for the last 12 months. The analysis showed that the brands that were more engaged on a variety of channels grew an average of 18 percent in revenue during the reporting period. In comparison, the companies that were least engaged suffered an average 6 percent decline in revenue. Starbucks, eBay, and Intel were all listed among the top 10 brands. This isn't an exact science, but consider it food for thought for brands that are considering engaging online.

In these examples, the noted brands listened to the conversation and then made actionable decisions to transform their organizations. The feedback has proven that those decisions were the right ones.

Establishing Continuity in the Global Landscape

In many large enterprise organizations, communicating is difficult without some level of governance. Global governance is a way to create accuracy, consistency, and repeatability in a process when teams are spread out far beyond just a functional group or business unit. The ability to work with global teams becomes imperative when establishing this governance and developing strategies to communicate with the social customer. In social media, this means establishing a formal set of guidelines that instruct sanctioned communicators on how best to represent the company externally. Guidelines and process documentation can include up-to-date lists of approved social media vendors, processes for being trained in social media or launching a new Facebook page, social media playbooks—including feature templates for building social media strategies, press releases. or even decision trees for crisis communication and PR disasters.

Some organizations are creating Digital Conversation Guides and distributing them to global teams in preparation for product launches, marketing initiatives, and in some cases events. A Digital Conversation Guide is a document that includes the following:

- A high-level overview of the product, event, or initiative to include important messaging; for example, product name, availability, functional specs, and featured speakers if it's an event

- Important dates; for example, when the press release hits the wires

- A list of assets to include important URLS, links to videos, blog posts, and online FAQ tagged with a consistent URL shortener like Bit.ly

- Agreed-upon hashtags, the corporate Twitter profile, as well as any other Twitter profiles that may be relevant

- Sample Facebook status updates and Tweets

The following is an example of a digital conversation guide of a company introducing a new laptop into the global marketplace:

Hello Social Media Practitioners & Community Managers,

On Monday, October 23, we are bringing to market Gadget —our new, ultrathin laptop which will be available in North America, Germany, UK, Spain, and Mexico. The Gadget will be available in most APAC markets in 2012. The press release hits the wires at promptly at 9:00 AM EST. Please wait to share any product-related information until after the press release goes live.

ACTION: Please help and support this product launch by amplifying it across your social networks and communities. Please remember to use your own voice and personal experience with the product.

Key Messages:

When communicating within your own micro communities, please remember the following:

- The Gadget is a high-performance and ultra-thin laptop that delivers a brilliant High Definition experience
- The Gadget outperforms all competitors with 12 hours of battery life
- The Gadget is perfect for the student, mom, and business professional who expects a high-quality video experience and long battery life

Assets:

- Blog post announcing the launch—http://bit.ly/jAoyR1
- Video Demos on Gadget.com—http://bit.ly/jAoyR2
- FAQ—http://bit.ly/jAoyR3
- Be sure to follow @gadget on Twitter and join/share the Facebook Fan

  Page —http://bit.ly/jAoyR4
- Hashtag: #gadget

Sample Tweets (please use your own tone/voice):

- So excited that we just launched the Gadget! http://bit.ly/jAoyR1—now I can watch 12 hours of HD movies! #gadget
- I travel all the time. With the new Gadget laptop, I can work on presentations during the entire flight http://bit.ly/jAoyR1 #gadget
- Interested in the Gadget laptop? Watch these cool demos! http://bit.ly/jAoyR1 #gadget

Sample Facebook Status Updates (please use your own tone/voice):

- Friends and Family—as you all know I have been working heads down on launching this new product! I am so excited that we just launched the Gadget! http://bit.ly/jAoyR1—now I can watch 12 hours of HD movies!

- Interested in the new Gadget laptop? Watch these cool demos on and join our fan page to get exclusive video content! http://bit.ly/jAoyR1

This simple email communication is an excellent way to communicate with global teams and get everyone on the same page for a specific product launch. It ensures a level of message consistency and also empowers employees who are sanctioned to engage externally with social media to communicate using their own voices.

To establish global continuity, it's important to facilitate bi-weekly or monthly social media integration meetings. It's imperative that global teams come prepared with case studies and programs to share best practices, key learnings, and successful failures, as well as discussions to improve collaboration and communication between the teams. Social media integration meetings also present an opportunity for corporate teams to pass down important messages that involve corporate governance initiatives. An email is effective; but an email, a collaboration forum, and consistent communication is more effective.

Standard Organizational Models for the Social Business

The external nature of social media is causing organizations to change the way they are organized internally. Entire textbooks, case studies, whitepapers, and dissertations have been written on this subject.

Two standard organization models exist in many companies today: centralized and decentralized. Figure 1.4 illustrates a centralized organizational model. This type of organization often operates in silos with the social media function usually reporting into corporate marketing along with corporate communications and marketing (web, channel, and retail). In this case, the strategy and execution is managed and governed without much collaboration with other business units, such as product organizations, customer support, and various geographies.

Organizations such as this usually are without social media guidelines or governance models, and rarely share best practices with other functional teams.

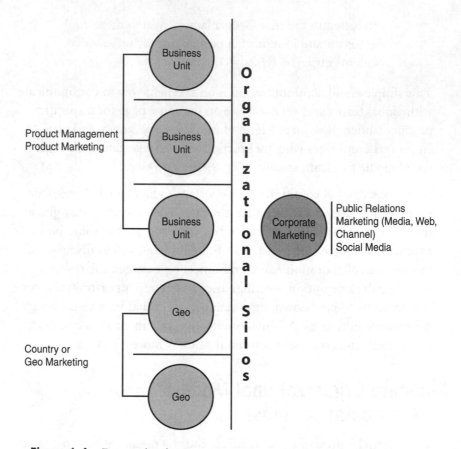

Figure 1.4 *A centralized organization operates in silos and reports into corporate marketing.*

This puts the teams outside of corporate marketing in a bind, especially if they want to use social media to engage with their customers. Centralized marketing organizations wrapped around silos and without governance models are bad for business because corporate marketing is silencing the teams that are closer to the product and customers.

A decentralized organization has other challenges. Figure 1.5 illustrates that the social media function reports into various business units and geographies. Depending on the company, there may or may not be a social media team reporting into corporate marketing. Many decentralized organizations are a natural result of silos; various business units, namely product organizations and customer support, start

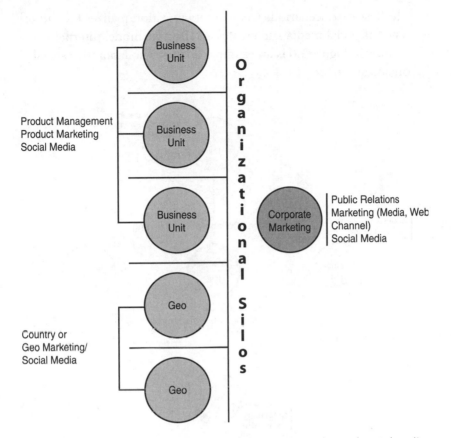

Figure 1.5 *A decentralized organization also operates in silos and social media is managed by a variety of different business units.*

using social media to communicate to their customers, troubleshoot customers' support issues, and even find sales leads. Because there is no governance, training, or internal communication, many of these business units are engaging blindly and some are making mistakes. Internally, this is causing a confusion of roles and responsibilities, with little to no collaboration. Organizations conflict because there is no clarity on who actually owns social media as a job function.

Externally, the end result is that the messages are often inconsistent with the company brand, and fragmented messages cause customer confusion. Also lost is the opportunity to partner with other business units to amplify the messages.

The best-case scenario is when an organization realizes the importance of social media and creates an effective model internally to address it. Figure 1.6 is an example of a fully collaborative social organization.

Figure 1.6 *A fully collaborative social organization empowers all business units and employees to engage and also has a governing body.*

In this case, there is a Social Media Center of Excellence (COE) team that reports into corporate marketing. The COE serves as a governing body and is responsible for creating governance models, facilitating best practice sharing, and training. Many times the COE is creating the brand strategy for social media. This type of organization is empowering and amplifying employees to engage externally regardless of their job function or what business unit they report into. In many cases, the business units (product organizations, customer support, human resources, sales, and various geographies) are responsible for the execution of social media programs, leveraging best practices, strategic support, and guidance from the COE.

Many COE teams are hiring global leads to ensure that there is global continuity and that regions are staying consistent with messaging, integrating with corporate, utilizing online assets, translating content, and driving other governance initiatives—for example, creating processes when a region wants to launch a Facebook page, Twitter account, or regional blog.

Intel has an excellent model that shows how an organization with close to 100,000 employees has addressed organizational silos through governance. Its Social Media Center of Excellence, which is responsible for creating and driving the global social media strategy, has the following tasks:

- Providing guidance and support for employees, product teams, and geographies when they want to engage externally with customers

- Managing, hiring, and recommending social vendors and agencies

- Facilitating biweekly and monthly meetings (the Social Media Integration Forum), with a goal of sharing knowledge across the organization

- Providing social media policies for the entire organization

- Providing, sharing, and governing social media best practices

- Training employees on new social tools

One example of the COE in action comes into play when a new employee joins an organization and wants to Tweet on behalf of the company. The COE should already have a process in place that addresses this particular scenario. The process might include a certain number of training hours before the employee starts. He or she might also get added to various communication forums, such as internal community groups and email distribution lists, in order to collaborate with the COE and other employees who are engaging with customers in social media.

Regardless of the organization model that a company adopts or naturally evolves into, there is always the question of "who owns social media?"

Who Really Owns Social Media?

One area of mass confusion and conflict is the functional ownership of social media. Marketing, public relations, and customer support teams might all think they should own it. Doing a quick search on Google for "who owns social media?" yields results from Mashable, Adage, Adweek, and hundreds of other blog posts. The short answer is that everyone in the organization owns a portion of social media. Jeremiah Owyang, partner at the Altimeter Group and former Forrester Analyst, often says, "Customers don't care what department you are in—they just want answers."

The job function of social media may well be governed beyond marketing or public relations, in the form of a COE to create the strategies, train employees, and write the policies. But it makes sense for some portion of social media to be executed and managed by the teams that are closest to the products. In some companies, social media responsibilities for a given product are the job of the product organization. This is an important factor to consider because these teams are the most familiar with the product, understand the value proposition for their customers, are familiar with the messaging, and usually have a higher degree of passion for it.

Unfortunately, the term *ownership* has negative connotations and normally prompts organizational conflict, resentment, and a decline in productivity. This is one of the challenges in working for a large company. However, it is important that today's business leaders adapt their organizations to better manage customer relationships even with the growing pains that result.

Taking the Next Steps

It's easy for someone to say, "Hey, you have to evolve your organization and tear down those silos." It's much harder to implement that change.

To start, business leaders need to think about the social customer and then begin transforming their organizational models and culture to best meet their needs. Starting slow is important, both because change like this doesn't happen overnight and because it will most likely be met with some opposition. The key is to start having those conversations today and get everyone involved. From marketing and public relations to IT and customer support, evolving to a social business requires a comprehensive change movement from every department.

Companies need to be prepared to fail, because it will happen. The important point to remember is to learn from those mistakes and avoid making them again. Document the failures, package them up like a case study, and share those experience across the organization. By doing so, it will help other teams understand what not to do in social media and increase the organizational intelligence at the same time.

Additionally, it's imperative to find someone in the organization who is willing to support the social movement. Send this person a meeting invitation, get on his or her calendar, and come equipped with data and case studies that will make it easy to support your initiatives and buy into social media.

In large organizations, it may seem impossible to find employees outside of PR/customer service who are willing to engage externally with customers. And for those who already are doing so, the challenge almost becomes an impossible task. Partner with the internal communications team and get on their editorial calendar when they send out company wide emails. Leverage the intranet, fight for home page real estate, and ask the question. Old-fashioned word of mouth doesn't hurt, either.

To establish global continuity, launch monthly social media integration meetings. Demand that the global team come prepared with case studies and programs, and be ready to share what corporate (or teams in the United States) are doing as well. Make it a point to find opportunities to share knowledge so that social intelligence can transfer easily from region to region. Leverage internal social networks or email distribution lists, and share articles, case studies, blog posts, or interesting Tweets. Use the regional leads to help amplify marketing messages in support of product launches, if applicable.

Organizations will always experience conflict, especially when it revolves around roles and responsibilities. It's important to address this challenge head on and document social media ownership from the beginning. Identifying roles, responsibilities, and ownership should be done in a collaborative environment in which all stakeholders are part of the decision-making process. Finally, be open to change. Customers, behaviors, products, and organizations all naturally change; be prepared to shift the balance of power and ownership of social media to others if it becomes more efficient and productive to do so.

In conclusion, it's been established that organizations need to evolve and change to meet the needs of the social customer. A portion of that change involves tearing down the silos that cripple a company's growth and innovation. At the core of this change are the people of the company. Change absolutely must start at the top from the CEO and work its way down. Employees from every department at every level from every group in every region need to feel empowered to try new things, talk and share internally, and apply best practices when they interact with customers in social media channels. Real evolution will happen only when everyone is aligned with this vision and is executing it daily. The next chapter discusses the technology that will aid companies in the quest to become a social business.

Surveying the Technology Supermarket

2

A strategy without execution is just a theory. And to execute, a company needs the right social media technologies.

Culture change and technology provide the foundation for success in all external social media efforts. Without these factors, a company is relegated to limited viewpoints and perspectives that will likely hinder organizations in their company effectiveness, innovation, and competitive relevance. Companies striving to become a social business require a very high level of collaboration across the organization.

Collaboration within the new business context of social media is defined as:

> To facilitate an environment of open sharing, create the necessary mechanisms for regular cross-departmental communications, encourage intellectual risk-taking, and respect honest failures while turning them into successful ones, all while keeping the social customer in mind.

Companies striving to become a social business require a very high level of collaboration across the organization.

Today, different departments claim ownership of various initiatives, programs, and business resources. Customer support usually owns the service relationship, the sales team may own the customer relationship management (CRM) initiatives, and information technology owns all the existing server assets. Organizations assign ownership partly to establish some semblance of responsibility, accountability, and governance. But what about some of those softer concepts of business operations? What about collaboration? Is this the domain of executives, department heads, or team managers?

Collaboration is owned either by everyone or by no one. It requires many willing participants to be open, to share, and to communicate. Just one unwilling team member or disengaged individual can break the entire system. And as much as this book discusses collaboration, technology is the means by which a company can operationalize it.

The market has clearly spoken. Consider all the development and marketing resources spent to compete in the very crowded "social technology" space. With Jive, IBM, Microsoft, Cisco, Adobe, and Citrix all vying as major players and a variety of startups close behind, a clear demand exists for tools and technologies that facilitate cooperative interactions and demonstrate a more efficient way to work together. The trick is finding the right solution to catapult the organization into a fully functional social business.

Collaboration and community solutions facilitate internal communication among employees, but publishing tools also are necessary for publishing content externally, streamlining workflows, and gathering metrics. Tools such as Sprinklr, Awareness, and the Syncapse Platform not only enable companies to publish content to multiple communications vehicles such as Facebook, Twitter, and YouTube, but they also provide a dashboard for metrics in one easy location. Additionally, most publishing tools allow companies to set up workflows to ensure, for example, that customer support teams are following up from a discussion on Twitter flagged by a community manager.

> Companies must also change and adapt their programs, process, and capabilities to keep up with technology innovation and the conversations within these networks.

Whether with collaboration software or publishing tools, it's important to keep a close eye on the external landscape of social media. In the coming years, Facebook, Twitter, and the mobile space will change dramatically. From a pure social business perspective, companies must also change and adapt their programs, process, and capabilities to keep up with technology innovation and the conversations within these networks—especially if internal tools are integrated with the external tools through APIs.

Choosing the Right Social Software

Many types of collaboration software solutions are on the market. With standard collaboration tools, Internet-based tools that live in the cloud, internal communities, wikis, and microblogging, the options are endless. The first step in facilitating collaboration across the organization is to examine what's available.

Jive

Jive is a social business collaboration tool with a wide array of features and capabilities. Jive's flagship product, Jive SBS (formerly Clearspace), combines collaboration software, internal community software, and a variety of social applications. Its features include the following components:

- A collaboration platform that enables employees to share information, make suggestions, and ask and answer questions in real time

- Customer support software that supports "customer-centric" communities with built-in support applications

- Social media monitoring software that enables brands to monitor external related conversations

- Company-branded communities (internal and external)

- Sales-enablement software that allows salespeople to immediately pool their knowledge about prospects, share reasons for winning or losing business, and collaborate with each other in real time

In 2008, storage and data management provider NetApp turned to Jive to create a community for its customers. The company launched a new branding campaign that included paid media initiatives and a new web site redesign. Through extensive online research, NetApp found that many customers and partners wanted a community to share knowledge, collaborate, and discuss business and technology concerns. The company launched a branded community using Jive's suite of products, with astounding results for a brand in the business-to-business (B2B) space:

- More than 9,000 registered users globally

- 78 percent of community users who are external (customers, partners, and technology experts)

- More than 900 discussions

- More than 50,000 page views of blog posts and whitepapers

Gartner, Inc., an information technology research and advisory firm, released its *Magic Quadrant for Social Software in the Workplace* in October 2010, which included an analysis on 23 social business software vendors in the space. Jive, along with Microsoft and IBM, was listed as a leader in the market.

Microsoft SharePoint

The most widely used collaboration software deployed in many organizations today is Microsoft's SharePoint product.

The advantage of using SharePoint is that it integrates with the broad suite of Microsoft products: Exchange, Outlook, and the rest of the Office products. Additionally, the software integrates comfortably with internal communities, dynamic/static web sites and content, and business intelligence, document management, and insights programs. SharePoint also has a well-established search functionality.

Intel uses SharePoint to manage internal collaboration among team members and across geographies. The company uses it to share files, marketing plans, editorial calendars, organizational charts, and other team documentation. SharePoint also helps Intel manage its internal digital training program, called Digital IQ. When fully deployed, SharePoint is an excellent tool that can facilitate collaboration across organizations, which is a key component of any social business.

IBM

The IBM social collaboration platform consists of three software packages, Lotus Connections, Lotus Quickr, and Lotus Sametime. Lotus Connections is a full-scale intranet, communities application, and social analytics platform all in one. It features commonly used capabilities such as blogs, file sharing, forums, wikis, and profiles for both internal and external use. Lotus Quickr is a team collaboration and enterprise content-management platform that can also be used for sharing files, hosting websites and communities, and maintaining content libraries. Lotus Sametime is an integrated, real-time communications services for voice, data, and video. This feature makes it easy to collaborate with colleagues, customers, and business partners.

Box.net

Box.net is a cloud-based file-sharing and content-management solution for individuals, small businesses, and large enterprise organizations. The company provides 5GB of free storage space for personal accounts and charges monthly fees for business accounts. A mobile version of the service is available for iPhone, iPad, and Android devices. Box.net is good for small companies that haven't yet invested in a full-scale social technology solution.

Tibbr

TIBCO has recently released tibbr, an enterprise-class social computing tool that lets users follow not only other people, but also information and events from deep inside their company's mission-critical systems.

Tibbr breaks business users free from one-dimensional social tools that focus on people by allowing information to be organized by subject or topic. The software enables users to follow and create subjects they are interested in, such as updates from accounting, urgent shipments from their supply chain, and sales orders. These status updates are posted onto a Facebook-style wall, along with the latest posts from whoever else in the company they're following. Feeds from external programs such as Facebook, Twitter, and Google Alerts can also be added; users can even use tibbr to read and respond to email.

Yammer

Yammer is an application that enables employees to microblog, share files, send direct messages, and create profiles all behind the firewall. It closely resembles Facebook's look and feel. It has the potential to replace entire intranets if fully deployed with all its capabilities. Yammer also can scale its functionality and can grow as a company grows and hires more people. In addition, Yammer's functionality includes the following:

- Private and public groups
- Company directory with search functionality
- Capability to tag topics
- Knowledge base
- Secure communications
- Open API so that other applications can be integrated

- Mobile application for iPhone, Android, and BlackBerry devices

Many top companies use Yammer for a variety of reasons, particularly because it's easy to deploy, is cost-effective, and is quickly scalable. AMD, for example, deployed its software mainly to engage with employees. The company uses the microblogging feature to encourage real-time discussions so that employees can ask questions at the quarterly WorldCast.

Yammer is growing quite rapidly. In November 2010, it raised an additional $25 million in new funding led by U.S. Venture Partners. The company has already added a variety of new features to increase its functionality, including polls, chat, events, links, topics, Q&A, and ideas. It also added a new Activity Feed that aggregates content about the employees' social graph both on and off the Yammer tool.

Although community and collaboration applications is one form of social technology to consider, platforms that facilitate communication via desktop sharing, conference bridge, and video capabilities are just as important.

Cisco WebEx Meeting Center

Whereas tools such as Jive, SharePoint, IBM, Box.net, and Yammer provide for document sharing and long-term collaboration, Cisco WebEx Meeting Center is best known as a conference bridge and a document/desktop–sharing video application. Used by three and a half million people every month, it has become synonymous with collaboration. WebEx is packed with a variety of useful features that help participants operate in an intuitive and efficient way. It's worth noting that WebEx has also evolved into a number of similar product variations, including WebEx Event Center, WebEx Support Center, and WebEx Training Center.

Collaboration ideas can be used in innovative new ways. In 2009, Seagate Technology used WebEx Event Center to create consumer buzz about a new solid state drive. The strategy for this B2B company was to go directly to the consumer.

Seagate decided to conduct a product launch via a live webcast that would give consumers direct access to Seagate's offices for demos, Q&A sessions, and so on. Seagate needed an online event-hosting solution that could accommodate many thousands of attendees, provide the highest-quality audio and video, and allow the event to be produced without any technical failures.

The Momentous XT webcast was a successful product launch: Several thousand people attended the online event, and the conversation went viral. Just a few short months later, Seagate continued to reap the benefits. The company sold thousands of devices on the day of the event and for months afterward. In fact, Seagate exceeded its sales goal by 300 percent.

Regardless of what reviewers and analysts say, business leaders must evaluate different social technologies and use criteria such as cost, implementation, integration with other technologies, and scalability before making the final decision. One such technology that is vital to integrate with collaboration tools is social listening software.

Social Listening Software Commoditized

Organizations have plenty of options for social media listening software applications. Social listening software monitors conversations in social media channels—blogs, forums, Twitter, and Facebook—based on a set of keywords. Users simply enter a keyword (such as a product or company brand), and the software reports on where these conversations are happening, the frequency of conversations, and even the sentiment. When using these tools, companies must think, beyond just listening. Listening without action is worse than not listening at all.

> Listening without taking any action is worse than not listening at all.

Radian6

Radian6 is a web-based social media listening platform that enables organizations to view and report on relevant conversations about a product or brand from around the social web. It offers a robust picture of brand-related conversations everywhere, including on blogs, Twitter, forums, and comments in YouTube.

Radian6 can also be used for enterprise collaboration. The software supports customized workflows by classifying posts (or external conversations), tagging them, and assigning them to other teams for follow-up and engagement and to see when a ticket has been closed.

Even more impressive is Radian6's innovation of the product. The company recently launched its Engagement Console, which enables users to not only listen to online conversations, but also to engage directly within the Radian6 platform. Radian6 also integrates with web analytic software such as Google Analytics, Omniture, and Web Trends.

A real-time scenario might look something like this. A community manager who is using Radian6 to monitor online conversations comes across a blog post giving false information about a technical product. The community manager can tag the post, adjust the sentiment, and assign it to a team member of the customer support organization. Customer support then gets flagged, addresses or comments on the blog post (or Twitter) directly from Radian6, and then closes the ticket. The community manager can see when the ticket is closed.

Radian6 also offers robust reporting that's useful for making data-driven decisions. The following reports are available:

- **Brand Overview**—A quick analysis of what's being said about the brand (volume, sentiment, share of voice, and any visible trends)

- **Sentiment Analysis**—An analysis that reports on the general sentiment toward a brand and how it changes over time

- **Influence Analysis**—A report that discovers which influential people are talking about the brand and what they're saying

- **Competitive Analysis**—An overview of how one product or brand is competing with another product or brand

- **Engagement Analysis**—An analysis that assesses how internal teams are interacting with the community

Lithium Social Media Monitoring (Formerly ScoutLabs)

Lithium Technologies, the leader in social customer solutions, acquired Scout Labs in May 2010 for good reason. For the most part, Lithium's product is similar to Radian6, with a few exceptions. Lithium's interface is easy to use, navigate, and pull reports from. This tool is much easier for first-time users.

What sets Lithium apart from other listening platforms is its automated sentiment analysis. Lithium uses natural language processing to assess the tone and sentiment of conversations. Even better, the system lets users override the analysis with their own assessment and then adds their input to the algorithm. For example, if the system automatically labels a particular conversation as negative but, after reading it, the user realizes that the conversation was more neutral, the user can change it. This happens a lot with slang. In other words, as more people use the tool, the system gets smarter and smarter.

Lithium also has a useful Frequent Words Analysis module. For example, when important topics emerge on the social web, they appear in the Frequent Word Analysis module, displaying the frequency of these terms in the conversation. This is extremely important from a crisis communications perspective because it enables organizations to stay ahead of the curve and equip themselves with actionable business intelligence before a situation spirals out of control. You can imagine the panic if terms such as "your brand" and "sucks" and "battery blew up" or "caught on fire" began to appear in the Frequent Word Analysis.

Lithium stands out among competitors for its breadth of social customer capabilities, as with its branded community platforms. Many big companies, including Sephora, Best Buy, and Hewlett-Packard, use the Lithium community platform, and the data it offers on the social customer is extremely valuable when coupled with external listening data.

Lithium's Customer Intelligence Center also can help companies identify the biggest influencers today and those who can potentially become advocates tomorrow. The tool delivers fine-grained details about consumer behavior and identifies the wants and desires of brand advocates so that a company can continue to deliver on its brand promise, excite the community, and potentially drive long-term business value. It's an additional service offering that provides data on customers, advocates, and influencers who are conversing about a given product or brand.

Meltwater Buzz

Meltwater Buzz, part of the Meltwater Group, might not be as well known as Radian6 or Lithium. However, with more than 100 million dollars in revenue, over 18,000 clients worldwide, and smart acquisitions in 2011, the Meltwater Group is certainly one of the strongest players in the online monitoring and social media listening applications space. What clearly differentiates them from others is their comprehensive suite of products that can be integrated into one platform. Not only do they have Meltwater Buzz, which monitors, analyzes, and reports on conversations in the social space, but they also have Meltwater News, which pulls similar data from traditional online media publications. Other tools within their suite include

- **Meltwater Press**—A media contacts database and press release distribution tool that pinpoints the most relevant journalists and influencers to send any press release or media pitch to by the content they publish using a new smart technology, Natural Language Processing

- **Meltwater Reach**—A platform that automates, optimizes, and provides more visibility into cross-channel, search-based advertising campaigns

- **Meltwater Drive**—An online collaboration environment that enables individuals to work more efficiently with their colleagues, partners, and clients

Additionally, in March 2011, Meltwater acquired JitterJam, a web-based Social CRM platform that combines social media, email, and mobile engagement with a contact database and the tools designed to turn social interaction into opportunities. JitterJam's capabilities are going to be fully integrated into the existing Meltwater Buzz product and bring a breath of new capabilities with focus on social profiling, social engagement, and tools for social marketing. The built-in deep analytics will measure the effectiveness of your communications and campaigns, the buzz around your brand, the growth of your database, and much more.

With this acquisition, Meltwater Buzz will be positioned as the first "online monitoring" application that has unique social CRM capabilities as a part of their core feature set. Meltwater is an Edelman Client.

Although social listening tools are excellent ways to help companies understand external conversations on third-party blogs, forums, and other sources, other technology providers manage, listen, and engage directly with the community in a brand's owned media channels, such as a brand's Facebook page, YouTube account, and Twitter stream. These tools are known as Social Relationship Management Applications.

Social Relationship Management Applications

Companies that own and manage multiple Facebook, Twitter, and YouTube accounts will have trouble publishing content, responding to comments, and pulling metrics reports efficiently. Having to log in and log out of multiple accounts each time to post content is not an effective use of time or money. Luckily, tools can help manage this process of quickly publishing content across multiple channels and also pulling metrics just as easily. Many social relationship management applications offer similar features, including these:

- Governance, workflow, and approval processes

- Capability to manage multiple conversations and publish across multiple channels, including Facebook, Twitter, LinkedIn, YouTube, foursquare, Gowalla, SlideShare, and various blogging platforms

- Robust one-click reporting

- Audience management and the capability to find influencers within owned media channels

- Message white labeling

- Report integration with common web analytics programs, including Google Analytics and Omniture

- Hosted solution

Sprinklr

Sprinklr is one of the industry's leading tools that manage social media programs. It has a robust analytics engine on the back end, which is one differentiator from its competitors. Sprinklr can pull reach and impression metrics across all social media channels and can rank a contact according to three different measurement criteria:

- Previous interactions
- Size and influence of networks
- Level of engagement

Awareness

Similar to Sprinklr, Awareness is a social media management software service. One of the main differences, however, is that Awareness enables marketers to respond to comments, delete comments from any of the social media channels, and flag comments for review by team members directly from the tool. The tool also can measure the sentiment of each comment made within the social channels. This is an extremely helpful feature because marketers can quickly respond to both negative and positive comments, as well as identify their detractors and advocates within the given community.

The Syncapse Platform

The Syncapse Platform is enterprise social media management software that helps brands acquire new fans and customers, build engagement to drive loyalty and sales, identify and motivate influencers and advocates, and measure ROI. The dashboard is very similar to both Sprinklr and Awareness. However, Syncapse also offers an additional data analytics package above and beyond measuring reach, impressions, engagement, and fan growth.

Syncapse's advanced analytics package reports on key measures that enable social marketers to understand performance of their programs. This includes values to gauge the return social marketing initiatives produce including Earned Reach, Earned Engagement, Earned Media Value, and Brand Favorability. This gives organizations the ability to evaluate social media spending in the same framework that they do traditional marketing spending, clarifying the value of social media marketing to senior executives within their organization.

Hearsay Social

Hearsay Social is a social media platform for organizations with many local branches, offices, or franchises. The product is designed to empower employees and branches to express themselves on local social media pages in an authentic voice, while ensuring compliance with corporate brand guidelines and industry regulations. Hearsay Social is a software-as-a-service (SaaS) platform with two views: corporate view and local view.

The corporate view for management includes compliance features for full message archiving, keyword flagging and filtering, workflow and approval capabilities for sound corporate governance, and FINRA/SEC/FTC and brand compliance. It also has the ability to publish content timely for campaigns and content suggestions, which can be dispersed by region or subregion as desired. Analytics also provide visibility across the entire organization's social media efforts with in-depth, real-time analytics, as well as the ability to drill down by region or subregion.

The local view for reps and branches includes streamlined content and simultaneous posting of suggested content and branded tabs (such as corporate marketing campaigns, contests, and videos) to Facebook, LinkedIn, and/or Twitter, with the ability to select and tailor to local preferences. It also has core social CRM features, including social contact management; it shows a 360-degree view of Facebook fans and friends, LinkedIn connections, and Twitter followers in a consolidated contact record that aggregates social network activities (such as posts, likes, comments, and tweets) and profile information.

What's important to realize with these social relationship management applications is the value proposition they bring to an organization: real-time analytics and content-publishing efficiencies. Real-time analytics help companies make effective data-driven decisions. If a certain community isn't responding well to certain types of content, these tools make it very apparent right away so that companies can make editorial changes to the content. Publishing efficiencies simply save time and free up companies to spend more time thinking about strategy instead of having to log in and out five different platforms every day.

Real-Time Analytics and Publishing Efficiencies

The benefit of using social relationship management applications is real-time analytics, which enables marketers to share the right content (or message) at the right time, to the right customer, in the right channel.

Whichever publishing tools are being used to publish content, it's important to keep a close eye on the data. Tools such as Sprinklr, Awareness, and the Syncapse Platform, among many others, are excellent tools for understanding, in real time, what types of content resonate with the community. The alternative means taking the shotgun approach and making assumptions, similar to the way traditional content is published on corporate web sites. Consider this quick illustration of social relationship management applications in action.

Imagine a brand that posts content to five different channels: two Twitter accounts, two Facebook pages, and one YouTube channel. Now let's say that a community manager looks at the analytics only at the end of each month when he pulls the analytics reports to share them with the broader marketing teams. The reports most likely aggregate page views, impressions, engagement (Retweets, Likes, Shares, and so on), and all the other important metrics. Senior management will almost certainly ask, "What content is working and what content isn't?" That data would certainly be easy to find, but it's useless at the end of the month because it's not actionable and the community is constantly changing. In other words, it's not actionable because the data is old.

On the other hand, imagine a brand that is very data driven about community growth, in the same scenario of managing five different channels. The only difference here is that the community manager looks at the content daily. The advantage here is actionable insights. Smart companies are using this data to influence editorial calendars and future content in real time. For example, if the person posting content is using a social media management tool, she will be able to see, almost instantly, which content is being shared, retweeted, liked, and clicked on the most. So if the content is a tutorial, the intuitive action is to share more tutorials. The end result is a more relevant customer experience and an increase in the content being shared, retweeted, liked, and clicked on.

Real-time analytics give tremendous insight into the times and days to post content within an existing community. Referred to as day parting, this is a popular practice among search engine marketers.

A 2010 study by Vitrue, a social media management company, titled *Managing Your Facebook Community: Findings on Conversation Volume by Day of Week, Hour and Minute,* identified when Facebook users are the most active on branded fan pages. Here are some key findings:

- Usage skyrocketed during three different times of the day, on weekdays at 11:00 a.m., 3:00 p.m., and 8:00 p.m. (all Eastern Standard Time).

- Wednesday at 3:00 pm EST was consistently the busiest day and time of the week.

- Sunday is not a good day to post content.

- Content posted in the morning performed better than content published in the afternoon (39.7% more effective in terms of user engagement).

- Content posted at the top of the hour performed better than content posted at other times.

By using real-time analytics and research provided by firms such as Vitrue, companies can publish content on Facebook at peak times when users are most active, to achieve maximum engagement.

The Future of External Social Technologies

Most of this chapter examined internal social technologies such as collaboration, listening, and social media management software. It's equally important to take a close look at external social technologies, to see how they are innovating, integrating, and merging. Why?

Because many companies today are using internal social tools that have open APIs and are synching them with Facebook, Twitter, and Google. Besides, what self-respecting book on social media would be complete without a hypothesis for the future of social technologies?

Innovation within the social landscape progresses at lightening speed. New business plans are written and proposed, venture capital is spent, and social apps are developed and released by the tens of thousands each month. The lucky few who achieve high levels of mass adoption, such as Facebook, Twitter, and foursquare, become part of an exclusive technology movement that influences the evolution of social media.

Many trends could really take off and change the social landscape for businesses everywhere. Here's our short list of things to plan for.

The Entire Internet Will Be Facebook

On *60 Minutes* in December 2010, Mark Zuckerberg told the world that users can do basically anything on Facebook that they can elsewhere online: shopping, searching, poking, stalking, chatting, blogging, emailing, collaborating, and more. And it's safe to say that the common question of "Are you on Facebook" is almost as popular as "Did you Google it?"

In 2010, comScore reported that Facebook finally surpassed Google in total time spent within its network, at 41.1 billion minutes over Google's 39.8 billion minutes in the month of August. Nielsen also released data showing that Americans spend nearly a quarter of their time engaging in social networks. Even more research from Nielsen found that the average time users spend using Facebook per month grew nearly 10 percent, topping seven hours. That's about 14 minutes per day and growing.

Facebook hit 500 million users in 2010 and is growing quickly. It's also building new products seemingly every day and is achieving high degrees of adoption. Given all these data points, Facebook is surely threatening other tools and technologies that at one time dominated a particular market segment:

- Search (Google, Bing)
- Chat (GChat, Yahoo! Instant Messenger)

- Email (GMail, Yahoo!, Hotmail)

- Blogging (Blogger, Wordpress)

- Groups and collaboration (Yahoo! Groups)

- Location-based services (Foursquare, Gowalla)

It's no wonder many executives fear the growth of Facebook. In fact, Yahoo! CEO Carol Bartz admitted at a New York City event in 2010 that the company's "greatest competitor probably is Facebook, more so than Google."

Facebook also is gaining widespread adoption of its Open Graph (API) platform, which enables third-party sites and applications to share information about users to provide a more relevant customer experience—even if that user has never been to those sites. In addition, during the Le Web conference in Paris in December 2010, Facebook's head of platform, Ethan Beard, told the audience that more than 250 million people globally are using the Facebook Connect ecosystem every month.

It wouldn't be a surprise if one day Facebook launched an enterprise version of its social network that companies could deploy behind the firewall to replace entire intranets and then potentially use Facebook Connect to replace enterprise single sign-on (SSO) solutions. This could pose a threat to companies such as Lithium and Jive that offer SSO as a core feature set of their community applications.

The point is clear: Facebook is well on its way to global dominance, and even Google can't stop it. The question is whether companies are ready to hop on for the ride.

Network Consolidation

The future of social media will surely hold several mergers and acquisitions. There are already many happening in the social media listening market, with Lithium acquiring Scout Labs, Attensity acquiring Biz360, and Meltwater acquiring JitterJam. But one acquisition that will likely gain the most attention is Google acquiring Twitter. And by the time this book is published, several more are sure to take place.

This will happen for several reasons. Google unsuccessfully launched two products: Wave and Buzz.

Google Wave is (or was) a software application positioned for real-time collaboration. First introduced at the Google I/O conference in May 2009, the product was discontinued less than a year and a half later; Google announced that it didn't plan to continue Wave as a standalone product. Wave failed for many reasons, mainly because it was just hard to use.

Buzz is Google's attempt to take share away from Facebook by integrating "the stream" into Gmail. The product enables users to share links, photos, videos, status messages, and comments organized in "conversations" and visible within the Gmail inbox. The product is similar to Twitter and Facebook, in that sense.

Buzz hasn't failed yet, but the product has caused plenty of problems for Google. When the product first launched in February 2010, it "opted in" every user of GMail to automatically "follow" those with whom they interacted with the most, via email or chat.

Many users felt their online privacy was violated, and class-action lawsuits were filed on behalf of every registered Google Buzz user, alleging violations of the Electronic Communications Privacy Act and other federal and state laws. Less than nine months later, the Associated Press reported that Google and the plaintiffs agreed to a settlement; starting in December, Google will start a fund worth $8.5 million to help pay for legal expenses for nonprofit organizations focused on privacy education.

With all this headache Wave and Buzz caused Google, it only makes sense that Google will go after Twitter. Twitter has a loyal community and has the mind share, infrastructure, data centers, and smart engineers already in place. And by acquiring Twitter, Google can only improve its search results. This is an important factor, considering that Facebook has partnered with rival search engine Bing to bring more relevant search queries based on a user's social graph.

This is relevant to social business because such an acquisition would position Google as a real-time collaboration tool and threaten the likes of Yammer and possibly IBM. Google can become a dominant player in the space if this acquisition happens.

Taking the Next Steps

When considering tools and technology, it's important to make strategic decisions and take a long-term view for any social business operation. Ultimately, missteps in this process can cause confusion organizationally, sour the adoption of social technologies, contribute to lost enthusiasm, result in political losses for an organization, and ultimately call into question the relevance of social media as a viable and measurable communication channel.

Technology is a critical part of any social media operation that hopes to scale and socialize its business. The following are some practical take-aways when considering technology integration and adoption of social applications.

Social Technologies

Every business is different. Each has its own individual processes, IT infrastructure, governance, and culture. And although this chapter covered many tools and technologies, it's important to remember that a solution that's a great fit for one company might be a disaster for another. Companies must take their time and test before making long-term technology decisions. The following are a few key questions to consider:

- Is the software scalable? As the company grows in size and infrastructure, can this technology also grow with it?

- Can this technology integrate with other internal databases and systems? This is especially important because many organizations are now employing social CRM programs.

- Does the company have the technical expertise to manage and deploy such technologies internally? If not, is a staffing plan being considered?

- Is IT involved in the decision of whether to use this technology? If not, it should be.

- Are other teams, regions, or business units already using the technology? If so, the company should understand the obstacles, if any.

Additionally, it's good practice to talk to others who have deployed the software within their organizations. Get their feedback and learn about what they like and don't like about the software. The more feedback it gets, the better equipped a company will be when making purchase decisions. Most collaboration vendors also offer free trials for 30 days. Spend time using an option and determining whether it's a good fit in terms of technology and culture.

Build a Listening Station: Listen and Act

Listening on the social web is one of the most important acts a company can take. Listening provides insight into what the community, customers, advocates, influencers, and press are saying about a given brand. This listening exercise should happen well before any external engagement takes place, or at least simultaneously.

What was once a cumbersome activity involving many disparate tools has given way to much more powerful technology solutions. This chapter touched on some major enterprise-class solutions, such as Radian6 and Lithium (formerly ScoutLabs), that are popular enterprise picks for social listening.

In 2010, Gatorade gained a lot of coverage by launching its Gatorade Mission Control Center inside its Chicago headquarters. It's basically a war room for monitoring the Gatorade brand (and competitors) in real time across various social media channels. The room features six LCD monitors, complete with data visualizations and dashboards (which are also available on employees' computers). Gatorade uses both Radian6 and IBM technologies.

For companies that cannot afford expensive enterprise-grade solutions, war rooms, and fancy dashboards, alternatives are available.

- Google still works. Google the brand name in quotation marks and use competitor keywords.

- Google Blog Search and Twitter Search. Although this method is completely manual and provides no historical trending data, it can still provide a quick snapshot of the sentiment of any brand in real time.

- The web-based tool Amplicate gathers the collective feedback from a community and reports both positive and negative sentiment on just about any topic. It also provides links to the actual conversations.

- Social Mention is a free social media monitoring tool that scrapes blogs, Twitter, forums, and the rest of the Web. It does lack reporting.

- Twitter Sentiment can pull just Twitter sentiment about any topic.

- Google Alerts also offers a subscription.

Social listening should be a major priority for any social business, but the actual *insights* from listening are where the true business value is found. It's not good enough to just listen—companies need to have a plan of action and a strategy for how to respond. Organizations that splurge on expensive listening and reporting subscriptions but fail to understand how to respond and react to this information are simply wasting valuable financial and human resources.

A social business is one that invests in technology that will allow it to collaborate, interact, share, and engage both internally and externally with customers. This chapter highlighted several well-known social technologies, but each company must determine which ones can grow and scale with the business.

A social business also takes into consideration the external landscape of social media. With the growth of Facebook, Twitter, Google, and mobile applications, companies need to understand the technical implications of what is happening externally and plan accordingly internally.

> A social business is one that invests in technology that will allow it to collaborate, interact, share, and engage both internally and externally with customers.

3

Establishing a Governance Model

It has been said that anarchism can be traced back to the origins of the ancient Chinese philosopher Laozi, the founder of the Taoism religion, more than 2,000 years ago. We've also seen anarchy arise throughout the world in 1642, 1720, 1749, and, most recently, 1993 during the crisis in Somalia.

Just as there was anarchy and political unrest in each of these key phases throughout history, there is anarchy in business today. The examples given appear to be more dramatic than what we see today in business, but modern-day organizational anarchy is causing unrest internally as it relates to transforming into a social business.

The modern-day cure for anarchy in business is a governance model. A governance model, also referred to as a governance policy, is a set of rules, policies, and procedures that companies create to manage social media internally. It addresses key factors, such as how to use social networks personally and professionally, training procedures, moderation of comments and user-generated content, and the basic tenets of disclosure and transparency.

As social networking and blogging began to catch on in 2000, employees began to blog about work issues. They shared their frustrations about the company; voiced their concerns about management, the stock price, and co-workers; and talked about (even promoted or defended) their company without disclosing that they worked there. They did this all within their personal social networks. Few problems arose because most people

> A governance model...is a set of rules, policies, and procedures companies create to manage social media internally.

weren't following blogs and reading these posts about issues at work. But as Facebook began to take over, much of that conversation shifted to the public Wall. The line between work and personal lives began to blur because many employees were also Facebook friends with their coworkers and managers. Additionally, many of these conversations began to appear in the search results.

Fast-forward a few years, and technology has given birth to tools such as Nielsen Buzz Metrics and Radian6, which listen to and report on conversations around the web about a particular topic. Departments such as human relations, legal, and public relations (PR) are now monitoring conversations going on externally about their brand and can identify employees who may be saying inappropriate things about the workplace on Facebook, Twitter, and just about everywhere else.

The consequences for such behavior are not going unnoticed.

In 2010, Dawnmarie Souza of Connecticut was fired from her job when she posted comments about her boss on Facebook. The trouble started when Souza expressed her anger on Facebook after claiming that her supervisor at the private ambulance company American

Medical Response (AMR) had denied her union representation after a customer complained about her work performance. From her home computer, she posted on her Wall, "Love how the company allows a 17 to be a supervisor." The term "17" is a code word medical professionals use to describe someone who is mentally ill. Souza also called her supervisor many derogatory names, but not once did she mention him personally. Friends and colleagues of AMR left several supportive comments on her Wall.

When management found out about her comments, Souza was fired.

Several other employees have been terminated from their jobs because of what they've posted on Facebook, Twitter, and personal blogs. Consider a few other noteworthy cases:

- Ashley Payne, a school teacher in Atlanta, was fired in 2009 after a parent complained about a photo of her on Facebook holding an alcoholic beverage.

- In 2009, Müller Tamás, an employee of the global telecommunications company Vodafone, was fired after he retweeted a T-Mobile post regarding network trouble.

- In 2009, Connor Riley, a student at the University of California, Berkeley, wasn't fired from Cisco—instead, she wasn't hired by Cisco as a result of what she posted on Twitter: "Cisco just offered me a job! Now I have to weigh the utility of a fatty paycheck against the daily commute to San Jose and hating the work." A Cisco employee captured this conversation and forwarded it to the hiring manager. The job offer was rescinded.

- In November 2008, New England Patriots cheerleader Caitlin Davis was fired from the team after she posted pictures of herself on Facebook posing next to an unconscious man covered with offensive graffiti, including two swastikas and crude drawings of male genitalia.

- In 2002, Heather Armstrong was fired from her job as a web designer and graphic artist at a start-up because she'd posted negative comments about her boss on her personal blog.

According to a study commissioned by IT staffing firm Robert Half in 2009, 54 percent of organizations in the United States have banned employees from using social media sites such as LinkedIn, Facebook, and Twitter during work hours. The study also found that 19 percent of companies allow social media use only for business purposes (such as LinkedIn for sales and staffing managers). Sixteen percent of companies allowed limited personal use, managed by controlled bandwidth via firewall restrictions in the IT department. The study was based on telephone interviews with more than 1,400 executives from companies with 100 or more employees.

What this study doesn't address is why companies are banning the use of social media during work hours. If employees are bashing a company or manager, sharing confidential information, or promoting the company without disclosing that they work there, it doesn't matter whether they're doing it during work hours or on their own time, right?

The case of Dawnmarie Souza and others will undoubtedly have an affect on employee privacy when it comes to social networking sites such as Facebook and Twitter. Problems like these can be avoided—or, at least, lawsuits can be prevented—if organizations have a governance policy that covers employee use of social media professionally and personally.

Having a governance policy not only addresses employees' use of social media in their personal lives, but it also establishes standards of practice for employees who use social media as part of their job. In some companies, all employees are encouraged to use social media (both within their personal networks and on company-managed social channels) to talk about the company, regardless of which department they're in.

The creation of social media policies and guidelines is the first step in creating a comprehensive governance model.

Crafting Social Media Policies and Procedures

The entire premise of this book is that organizations need to open up their firewall, evolve into a social business, and allow employees to engage with customers. To do so, a level of governance must be in place to avoid some of the embarrassing situations discussed earlier and, more importantly, to protect, inform, and educate the organization in its entirety. One element of governance is a social media policy, which is a company's first line of defense in mitigating risk for both the company and the employee. A nondisclosure agreement (NDA), a general confidentially agreement, or a few paragraphs added to the employee handbook on ethics is simply not enough.

Although it's not as sexy and engaging as a Facebook application, a social media policy is much more important. First and foremost, organizations need to communicate with their employees and let them know the risks of using social media. They also must inform employees that the right to privacy when posting public content is nonexistent. Posting questionable or obscene content on the social web also can have serious consequences, up to and including termination and legal trouble.

Additionally, companies shouldn't use a social media policy as a scare tactic for employees. Instead, the policy should be used as a tool that communicates openness and transparency for everyone who engages on behalf of the brand within social media. It's important here to reiterate that, according to the Edelman Trust Barometer, consumers not only trust "people like themselves," but they trust employees of a company *even more*. This data alone is enough for organizations to start thinking about empowering their employees to engage with customers.

> Social media policy ...should be used as a tool that communicates openness and transparency for everyone who engages on behalf of the brand within social media.

It's imperative to collaborate with other business units when crafting a social media policy and to include participation or input from marketing (or a social media team), PR, customer support, legal, information technology (IT), and various business units. As mentioned in Chapter

1, "Human Capital, Evolved," if social media resides within a centralized function, this is one of its core areas of responsibility.

Two important factors must be considered when writing the policy. The first is that the policy must protect the organization by all means possible. Second, it should empower employees to engage externally with the community without fear of backlash.

Consider an excerpt of the publicly facing Intel Social Media Policy that addresses employees' use of social media both personally and professionally (dated November 2010):

> When You Engage:
>
> Emerging platforms for online collaboration are fundamentally changing the way we work, offering new ways to engage with customers, colleagues, and the world at large. It's a new model for interaction and we believe social computing can help you to build stronger, more successful business relationships. And it's a way for you to take part in global conversations related to the work we are doing at Intel and the things we care about.
>
> If you participate in social media, please follow these guiding principles:
>
> - Stick to your area of expertise and provide unique, individual perspectives on what's going on at Intel and in the world.
> - Post meaningful, respectful comments—in other words, no spam and no remarks that are off-topic or offensive.
> - Always pause and think before posting. That said, reply to comments in a timely manner, when a response is appropriate.
> - Respect proprietary information and content, and confidentiality.
> - When disagreeing with others' opinions, keep it appropriate and polite.
> - Know and follow the Intel Code of Conduct, the Intel Privacy Policy.

The Intel Social Media Guidelines also link to Intel's privacy policy, called the Intel Code of Conduct, which it has also made public.

In 2009, Coca-Cola released a very simple social media policy that featured 10 principles for employees who engage externally:

1. Be certified in the Social Media Certification Program.

2. Follow our Code of Business Conduct and all other Company policies.

3. Be mindful that you are representing the Company.

4. Fully disclose your affiliation with the Company.

5. Keep records.

6. When in doubt, do not post.

7. Give credit where credit is due and don't violate others' rights.

8. Be responsible to your work.

9. Remember that your local posts can have global significance.

10. Know that the Internet is permanent.

Several years ago, before the acquisition of Sun Microsystems by Oracle, the Sun social media policy simply read, "Don't be stupid." It probably wasn't the smartest, most comprehensive policy, but it does show the level of trust Sun had in its employees.

Every social media policy is different, determined by the organization's culture and value system. However, some key points should always be present, including the rules of engagement for on- and off-domain web properties and the company's moderation guidelines.

"Rules of engagement" simply refers to actual employee engagement (or behavior) within social channels. An on-domain property is a corporate blog or community (a site that is operated and controlled 100 percent by the company); off-domain properties are sites such as Facebook, Twitter, YouTube, and external (third-party) blogs. When employees decide to engage in off-domain properties, it's important that they remain completely transparent about where they work and what their intentions are.

Transparency and Disclosure

Most people are smart and understand that they need to be transparent while engaging with consumers. Transparency is common sense. It simply means that employees and companies should always be honest and disclose everything (when leaving comments on a third-party blog, tweeting, launching unbranded microsites, and so on). Unfortunately, transparency can be overlooked or forgotten.

Sony learned this lesson the hard way. Back in 2006, the company launched the blog "All I Want For Xmas Is A PSP" but forgot to tell the world that Sony was behind it. Whether Sony simply forgot or purposefully tried to deceive the public and manipulate purchase intent is irrelevant. The company was being dishonest. To this day, Sony hasn't apologized for its mistake. It merely deleted the entire blog and acted as if it had never happened. That's one reason Sony won "The Best Fake Blog of 2006" award, given by *The Consumerist*.

Being transparent isn't hard to do. As long as people are disclosing that they're employees of a given company in their bios, within the comments of a third-party blog, and somewhere on their personal blogs, that should be enough. The team at Dell uses consistent nomenclature in naming their Twitter accounts (as in @RichardatDell, @LionelatDell), to easily identify themselves as Dell employees.

The policy should also include some language that covers what employees should be talking about as it relates to their expertise. In other words, if there's a conversation online in a forum about virtualization and data centers, it would make sense for an expert in virtualization to participate in the conversation, not someone from marketing. Employees have to add value to the conversation. If they can't, they should think twice about interrupting.

Moderation

The social media policy should also explain moderation guidelines. It's important for internal teams to not only understand these guidelines, but also set expectations within the community. Moderation includes comments left on corporate blogs and communities, as well as social networking sites such as Facebook via the fan page.

Intel's social media policy takes a "good, bad, and ugly" approach—that is, Intel accepts comments from the community that are good and bad, but not ugly. Good comments are self-explanatory. Bad comments might be a little aggressive and critical, and might come from a competitor. Ugly comments usually have derogatory statements, curse words, or simply spam content. When receiving ugly comments, it's good practice to notify the commenters, explain the policy, and then ask if they would like to resubmit their comment for consideration.

Two types of moderation are used: pre-moderation and post-moderation. With pre-moderation, before a comment goes live on a blog, it must go through an approval process with either an employee or an outsourced vendor. With post-moderation, comments go live immediately but can be deleted in the future if they violate policy. In thriving communities, members usually self-moderate and community managers rarely need to intervene.

Many companies today use post-moderation for their corporate blogs and communities. For user-generated content, a pre-moderation policy is used mainly to protect the organization from illegal or copyright material being posted on a branded site.

Moderation is an important characteristic of any social business, but having an escalation process for every external property (such as a micro site or Facebook) that allows comments or user-generated content is vital, especially when dealing with a crisis communication situation.

In May 2010, an activist group opposed to minerals mining in the Democratic Republic of Congo inundated Intel's Facebook page with comments asking for Intel's support of the Conflict Minerals Trade Act. This particular congressional bill was created to restrict the import of minerals from war-torn countries.

Intel responded by first deleting many of the activists' comments and then turning off the ability to comment for everyone. This probably wasn't the most effective first reaction, but it's understandable why the company chose to do this. Intel wasn't prepared to handle this from a crisis communications perspective.

To Intel's credit, it eventually reinstated the commenting function on Facebook and posted an official announcement on its Corporate Social Responsibility Blog. Kelly Feller, social media strategist, also posted the following comment on Oregonlive.com in response to a critical blog post:

> Today we at Intel were reminded about the power of Facebook— and the effect of seemingly small acts, by both passionate advocates and by well-meaning social media employees.
>
> We at Intel would first like to apologize for deleting some comments and temporarily shutting down our Facebook page for comments for a brief period of time this morning. I can tell you that our intent wasn't to silence the valuable opinions of our Fans. In trying to remain sensitive to all our Fans, we often delete messages that are political in nature or could be perceived as spam (messages with the exact same language repeated, instead of ongoing conversation or dialogue). However we should have been more sensitive to the very important topic at hand. For that we are deeply sorry.

It's safe to assume that the next time a potential crisis like this happens to Intel or one of its social media properties, the company will be prepared to act. This is why it's imperative to be proactive in creating moderation strategies for both on- and off-domain properties and to have a crisis communication plan, just in case.

What's more important than just having a crisis communication plan is to ensure that the entire organization is trained and understands the escalation policy in case an employee comes across a potential crisis on the social web.

Training and Organizational Intelligence

When enlisting in the United States Marine Corps, recruits must first attend the Marine Corps Recruit Depot, also known as Boot Camp. They spend the next 12 weeks being trained in military etiquette, Marine Corps history, hand-to-hand combat, infantry, weapons familiarization, the Uniformed Code of Military Justice, basic grooming standards, and drill (marching). They also have to exercise three to four hours a day to burn body fat, build muscle, and improve their metabolism.

Similarly, in the National Football League, teams normally begin training camp in late July to begin preparing for the regular season at the beginning of September. That gives coaches and players about three months to train, learn the offensive and defensive playbooks, get in shape, get to know each other personally, and start playing as one cohesive unit.

Just as the military and the NFL are constantly trying to get more intelligent, companies should build a culture of learning. Innovation in the social media space is moving faster than anyone could have ever anticipated, and it's not slowing down. Tools are changing, networks are merging, start-ups are being acquired, and consumer behavior is constantly evolving. Companies need to stay ahead of the game, and, to do this, they must get smarter. This requires training and organizational development. The evolution to a social business doesn't happen overnight. It's not a button that can just be turned on. It's a process that can take years and that requires training and intelligence companywide.

> The evolution to a social business doesn't happen overnight. It's a process that can take years and that requires training and intelligence companywide.

In 2009, Intel created a digital training program called Digital IQ. This was a series of PowerPoint training sessions meant to equip not just digital marketers, but anyone within the organization who wanted to participate in social media, with the tools necessary to engage intelligently. Digital IQ was built on a university model of 100- to 400-level courses. All members of Intel's sales and marketing organization are required to take a series of digital marketing courses based on their roles. Those roles, with closer responsibilities to the web, are required to complete higher level 300- to 400-level course work.

Training topics include these:

- Basics of digital marketing
- Social media tools (Twitter, blogs, community platforms, Friendfeed, Facebook, and so on)
- Ways to be more conversational on the social web
- Geography-specific training about social networking in specific countries
- Legal and ethics overviews
- Search marketing

The social media team partnered with the internal communications team to make employees aware of the training. In some organizations, training became mandatory. The point is that Intel knew it had to get smarter. It saw the external landscape shift and wanted to make sure it wasn't left behind.

What's important in training is that material needs to be updated regularly. Many employees who sign up to engage in social media are doing so above and beyond their normal job responsibilities. They might spend an hour or two each day on Twitter, but the rest of the day they might be optimizing a data network or coding in Java. They don't have enough time in their day to stay up-to-speed on the changes to the tools they use daily. They need guidance and *actionable* training. Training in theory with topics such as "Why Social Media" might be an effective way to recruit new employees, but it's not sustainable in the long term. When employees complete a training module, they should know what to do next. The team in charge of the training curriculum must consider revising the training program at least every two to three months or when something significant happens in social media (such as a merger or acquisition).

Another form of training involves collaborating with other companies to get a better understanding of how they are deploying social media and the best practices they're using.

Noncompetitive Collaboration

Every organization is different. Every customer is different. And the way each business communicates with its customers is different. There's no single, or right, way to engage with customers—it's a dynamic relationship that changes from one customer to another.

Often organizations operate with tunnel vision: They do something one way because they think it's working. They rarely step out of their comfort zones and try new and innovative things. They might read a few articles, blog posts, or case studies that nudge them to evolve their process, but that rarely makes a difference.

Companies need to communicate with other companies to increase their social intelligence. Obviously, it doesn't make wise business sense for Intel to get up close and personal with AMD and discuss which community platform they use or how they're measuring social media.

This is about noncompetitive collaboration. It's a simple concept that means companies should collaborate with other, noncompetitive companies and share best practices. The Social Media Business Council, formerly the Blog Council, is one organization that is striving to help Fortune companies achieve this. Council members meet regularly, in person and on conference calls, to discuss, collaborate, and share best practices on challenging issues facing social media teams in large organizations. Here's a brief highlight of discussions (taken directly from the website www.socialmedia.org):

- How are you organized: PR or social media?
- How do you handle negative comments?
- What do you do when your blogger leaves?
- What is your process for setting up a blog or community?

Members of the Social Media Business Council also collaborate on projects that they make public for anyone to use:

- Metrics and the ROI of blogging
- Disclosure policy toolkit
- Benchmarks survey

Whether it's the Social Media Business Council or simply companies reaching out to colleagues in different companies, it makes perfect sense for companies to learn from each other. Noncompetitive collaboration is a great way to gain insight, gather feedback, and talk through some of the challenges that social media can bring to an organization.

Social Media Executive Councils

Many organizations are creating executive councils or forums to address social media. It's a meeting where key decision makers in the organizations discuss social media, and it covers a wide array of topics that are relevant to the business. At these meetings, everyone involved in social media can communicate, share best practices, give updates, and learn from each other. For example, Intel created a social media Integration forum, a once-a-month meeting where global marketers and communications teams discuss best practices of social media within their regions. Agenda items usually include these:

- Guest speakers
- Vendor presentations
- Social media program overview
- Quarterly business review (QBR)
- Training and updates

Many times, these meetings are also a place where social media teams and governing bodies can roll out new initiatives for other teams to adopt and use (such as Global Listening programs metrics models, Facebook and Twitter strategies, and more) and also provide guidance and feedback to teams that are starting to launch social programs. Cisco hosts a monthly Social Media Roundtable meeting to discuss recent successes and failures within social media programs and discuss ways to improve and optimize existing programs. The end result is a smarter organization. Usually these forums are facilitated by a team member from the social media team.

Additionally, these meetings can be used to ensure a strong level of collaboration and consistency across the organization. In some cases, anyone who engages in social media may be invited to a meeting to discuss a particular product launch happening in the future. To ensure consistency in the social marketplace, teams will share specific information such as common hashtags for the product, location of online video assets, press release dates, sample product messaging, and sample tweets and Facebook updates. The end result of such meetings is that once the product launches, everyone is equipped with the appropriate information to begin sharing details of the launch within their own micro-communities.

Another form of social media collaboration can also happen at the executive levels. These meetings usually include senior level managers in marketing, public relations, customers support, IT, operations, and finance. The purpose of these committees is usually to discuss the overall vision of social media and how it can drive business value for the organization. Budget allocations to social media and organizational changes are also topics that are normally discussed. These committees also go through approval and selection processes and make decisions about:

- Agency selection and RFP process

- Technology vendors to use internally

- Approve/disapprove social media marketing plans presented by junior staff team members

Taking the Next Step

When crafting social media policies, it's a good idea to keep it simple, especially if the policies will be public. If employees see too much fine print and legal jargon, they might decide not to engage because they won't know exactly what they're agreeing to. It's fine to have more comprehensive internal policies, as long as they don't contradict the external guidelines.

Remember to get everyone involved when creating the policy. PR and marketing will most likely be the drivers of the policy because most of what they do revolves around external engagement. IT and the privacy team will need to look at the policy to ensure that it complies with all federal and state privacy laws. Customer support might or might not be involved, depending on that department's level of engagement on the social web. Finally, legal will want to approve the policy, to ensure that it's protecting the organization.

Many tools can help you get started. Simply Google "social media policy templates" to see a wide variety of starting points. The Intel Social Media Guidelines are also a good model to follow. Policytool.net is another free tool that can help create social media guidelines. After only five minutes spent answering 12 questions, here's a quick excerpt of its recommendation (example only):

> *Smart Business, Social Business* Social Media Policy
>
> This policy governs the publication of and commentary on social media by employees of *Smart Business, Social Business* and its related companies ("Smart Business, Social Business"). For the purposes of this policy, "social media" means any facility for online publication and commentary, including, without limitation, blogs, wikis, and social networking sites such as Facebook, LinkedIn, Twitter, Flickr, and YouTube. This policy is in addition to and complements any existing or future policies regarding the use of technology, computers, email, and the Internet.
>
> *Smart Business, Social Business* employees are free to publish or comment via social media in accordance with this policy. *Smart Business, Social Business* employees are subject to this policy to the extent that they identify themselves as a *Smart Business, Social Business* employee (other than as an incidental mention of place of employment in a personal blog on topics unrelated to *Smart Business, Social Business*).
>
> Before engaging in work-related social media, employees must obtain the permission of Michael Brito.
>
> Publication and commentary on social media carries similar obligations to any other kind of publication or commentary.
>
> All uses of social media must follow the same ethical standards that *Smart Business, Social Business* employees must otherwise follow.

The policy also addressed key areas, including

- Setting up social media channels

- Protecting secrets

- Protecting your own privacy

- Being honest and transparent

- Respecting copyright laws

- Respecting the community

- Addressing controversial issues

- Admitting to mistakes

- Thinking about the consequences

Eric Schwartzman, consultant and coauthor of *Social Marketing to the Business Customer*, provides a free template for organizations to download and use (www.ericschwartzman.com/pr/schwartzman/social-media-policy-template.aspx).

An immediate next step is to begin developing a training program that can be rolled across the organization. It's good practice to partner with human resources or the learning and organizational development teams because they likely have access to the tools and resources needed to build a training curriculum. They can assist in making the training program available online via a learning management system (LMS) such as SharePoint or Intelex. The most important takeaway is to ensure that the training stays up-to-date and consistent with the dynamic nature of the social landscape.

If an organization has the financial resources available, it's recommended to join the Social Media Business Council. All members of the council have access to other brand marketers. The sharing of best practices, concerns, and challenges is encouraged, and it's done in a safe environment. Other options include simply reaching out to other marketers in the enterprise via Twitter or LinkedIn and requesting a meeting. LinkedIn also has a library of enterprise marketing related groups that are filled with dynamic discussions and sharing, with some being open for everyone to join and others requiring approval. Last, Jeremiah Owyang, an analyst at Altimeter Group, publishes an excellent resource on his blog titled "people on the move in the social media industry" (see www.web-strategist.com/blog/category/on-the-move/). From there, Googling the names to acquire contact information is easy to do. Most enterprise marketers are open (and even thrilled) to share best practices with others on the phone or over a cup of coffee at the local coffee shop.

> Having an effective governance policy that addresses key principles and the basic tenets of disclosure and transparency is imperative in maximizing the effectiveness of any social business.

Social media executive councils might or might not have executives involved. In either case, it's important to first define the objective of the council and then invite the appropriate persons. Starting small is important to avoid group think. As the organizations evolve and change, so will the council; and many times, the council will be in the driver's seat facilitating organizational change.

Evolving to a social business isn't easy. All companies have to deal with at least a few growing pains. One is the concept of employees running wild and posting obscene or unprofessional comments within their social networks. The other is employees who are sanctioned to do social media making stupid mistakes that can also get them in trouble. Having an effective governance policy that addresses key principles and the basic tenets of disclosure and transparency is imperative in maximizing the effectiveness of any social business.

4

Embracing the Social Customer

In a perfect real-world scenario, this book is meant to mirror, in chronological order, the natural evolution into a social business. That is, a business undergoes a cultural change and a shift in the way it operates:

Tearing down silos and communicating effectively across the organization → adopting social technologies that foster communication globally → instituting governance models that emphasize smart participation on the social web → employing tactical considerations that address the social customer.

People have always been social, even before the Internet. Sharing experiences with others about the brands, products, and services that they love or hate comes naturally. The difference today is that the social customer now has a voice that travels well beyond the living room. The social customer is influential and isn't afraid to blog about negative experiences, share thoughts on Twitter, and post critical comments within status updates on Facebook. Some customers even spend hours writing well-formed critical product reviews on Consumer Reports, CNET, Epinions, Amazon, and Yelp. The end result of all these conversations happening in the social space is that every review, rant, criticism, praise, opinion (positive or negative), blog post, and tweet is appearing in Google search engine results—and has been for many years now. Companies might face a reputation-management problem when others see criticism in the search results when searching for a brand or product.

> **The difference today is that the social customer now has a voice that travels well beyond the living room.**

Companies need to embrace social customers and learn how to work with them collaboratively. This starts with a social media practitioner, the point person in any organization who establishes, fosters, and guides conversations with customers across the social web.

The Value of a Social Media Practitioner

The social media practitioner is potentially any employee with sanctioned authority to represent the brand or the product or service on the social web. The social media practitioner is essentially responsible for interacting and engaging with the social customer. This person might or might not have "social media" in the job title and could be a customer support agent or an engineer. Social media practitioners are mainly responsible for managing the daily operations of a community or routing service requests, product insights, or sales inquiries to the appropriate subject matter experts or departments. Social media practitioners might also be responsible for collecting actionable intelligence, insights, and reports, as well as making specific recommendations for editorial changes to corporate blogs and communities based on those insights.

Social media practitioners can include the CEO, the chief marketing officer (CMO), or even the information technology (IT) analyst who just started with the company. Often the title "social media practitioner" is synonymous with "community manager." This depends on how the company is organized internally.

The value of social media practitioners is twofold. First, customers see them as trusted sources of information, more so than corporate communications and advertising personnel. Why? Because people trust other people like themselves. This was discussed in Chapter 1, "Human Capital, Evolved," when referencing the Edelman Trust Barometer. Second, the social media practitioner is the company's first line of communication with the social customer, so the trust factor is an extremely important attribute.

Social media practitioners are the human link between a company and its customers. Because this is such an important responsibility, companies need to consider several criteria before hiring an employee for this role.

Hiring Social Media Practitioners

The phenomenon known as the "social media expert" is largely a myth. Avoid individuals who promote themselves with such a label. The very nature of this space involves constant change and adaptation. It is said that true knowledge is found in understanding that there's always much to learn, and the same is true for social media.

That being said, it's still important for companies to hire and train social media practitioners and help them develop expertise about both the brand and social media technologies and best practices. When hiring specifically for a social media practitioner, it's important to look for certain qualities in candidates:

- **A passion for social media**—A good social media practitioner knows about popular new social technologies and has an ongoing interest in news related to the progression of social media and its application to business. He or she is also passionate about customers and the brand or product.

- **A people person**—Look for someone who can communicate effectively online, offline, and in blog posts, in 140 characters or less. He or she must also be able to communicate the value of social media to senior management.

- **Strategic thinking**—The candidate must be able to set measurable goals and look beyond social media when creating marketing plans. The ability to see the big picture is important.

- **Effective collaboration skills**—Communication skills and effective sharing of ideas can make a significant impact across the company in various business units and geographies.

- **Analytical thinking**—The candidate must be able to understand various methods of tracking the effectiveness of external social media engagements, and then extract key and actionable insights to use for future plans.

Whether a company is hiring social media practitioners or simply empowering and training existing employees, a governance model must provide direction and guidance when creating social media profiles, specifically with Twitter.

For example, when engaging with social customers on Twitter, it's absolutely vital to be 100 percent transparent in all communications with them, and this starts with disclosure. It's good practice to disclose the nature of the relationship between the practitioner (the employee, contractor, or agency) and the company represented somewhere in the bio. This can be as simple as stating, "I work for company X, but these opinions are my own." At all costs, social media practitioners also should avoid spamming the community with one-way

> When engaging with social customers on Twitter, it's absolutely vital to be 100 percent transparent in all communications with them, and this starts with disclosure.

marketing messages and promotions. An overly commercial message is a very easy way to convince the social customer of your irrelevance. It may even spark a groundswell movement of criticism, which is never good for any brand.

Perhaps one of the best ways to find qualified talent is to leverage the collective networks of those who already have a solid grasp of the social media space. Cisco is a good example of a leading-edge social media organization that exemplifies this behavior. Candidates there are sourced internally from the networks of existing staff.

After a company has identified, hired, and trained its social media practitioners, the next step is to determine how those people should represent themselves on the social web and establish a social media profile to engage with the social customer.

Corporate Profiles Versus Personal Profiles

When employees first began using social media professionally, they were tweeting and blogging about anything and everything. Some employees were disclosing where they worked, and some weren't. Some were using the corporate logo as their profile picture, and others were using their own head shots. Others were spamming anyone and everyone with one-way marketing messages and promotions. The social web was basically a free-for-all—and the source of major internal headaches for senior management. Few companies established governance models and began to think through tactical approaches to external engagement.

Specifically, few companies considered the management and governance of social media profiles and, more importantly, what happens when employees decide to leave a company after they have built significant brand equity within those social profiles.

One example is the Twitter profile. Three types of Twitter profiles have evolved in the last few years: personal, corporate, and hybrid.

A personal profile is self-explanatory: It's used for personal reasons (to share relevant content with friends, ask and answer questions, promote one's own content, ramble, and in some cases build a personal brand). If employees are using a personal profile to talk about the company they work for, they should disclose that they are employees of that company. This is standard practice, and most people are doing this today. Additionally, most personal profiles link to a personal blog, Facebook page, or LinkedIn profile.

A corporate profile usually has the trademarked name as the Twitter handle (as in @Intel, @Dell, and @Adobe). The look and feel of this profile is company branded and matches the corporate identity of the organization. Often the logo serves as the profile photo. Much of the content shared on a corporate profile is specific to company-related news (announcements, staff hires/departures, press releases, product launches, press briefings, quarterly earnings, and so on). Additionally, companies are creating Twitter profiles specifically for products such as @Photoshop, which are used just to share product-related content and interact with their community. Customer support usually has its own corporate profiles as well. For instance, Adobe has @Adobe_Care, used to solve customer support inquiries across all product lines.

Hybrid profiles come in a variety of shapes, sizes, and colors. No set standard or existing nomenclature is used; a hybrid profile embodies characteristics from both the corporate and personal profiles. One that really stands out is Scott Monty's Twitter account. Monty runs digital marketing for Ford Motor Company. A close examination of his profile reveals that he uses elements from both a corporate profile and a personal profile. His Twitter background is completely branded Ford, so at first sight, it looks like he is either a Ford enthusiast or an employee. As his profile photo, Monty uses a picture of himself with a Ford logo at the bottom. He fully discloses that he works for Ford, and much of his daily interaction involves evangelizing about the Ford brand, interacting with his community, or answering Ford-related questions. Monty links to his personal blog, where he writes mostly about social media marketing and not so much about Ford.

The question "What happens when Monty decides to leave Ford?" suddenly turns into a serious business concern, especially because he has almost 50,000 followers and has built significant brand equity for Ford and himself. That's why it's important for organizations to think about the long-term implications when appointing external spokespeople and empowering social media practitioners to engage online. Companies must consider two issues to protect themselves:

- Establish a governance policy that addresses personal and company profiles. More importantly, for personal profiles, companies must determine how much of company resources can be used to promote their growth and expansion.

- Empower more than one employee to be external spokespeople for the brand. Dell has done an outstanding job of this over the last five years by empowering multiple employees to engage externally and even standardizing their Twitter accounts (as in @richardatdell, @chrisatdell, @deniseatdell, and @manishatdell).

Empowering more than one person to engage with the social customer is good practice because it potentially solves a few problems before they even arise. First, although these Twitter accounts are personal profiles, the standard nomenclature makes it naturally transparent where Richard, Chris, Denise, and Manish work. In addition, if one of them decides to leave Dell, the company would face minimal impact because the others would be able to take up the slack and continue to engage with the community.

One of the most common ways for companies—specifically, social media practitioners—to address the social customer is through customer support. Most conversations that involve the social customer are complaints and concerns about a company's product or services—and maybe even the support department itself—so this is a natural first step.

Integrating Customer Support into Social Media

Obviously, social customers have a voice. And since the birth of channels such as Twitter, they also have an audience, some big and some small. Regardless of the audience size, these consumers have no problem slamming companies that offer substandard customer service or products. Even worse is that many of these critical conversations on Twitter, blogs, and review sites appear in search results for others to read—and they live on the Internet forever. This new, disruptive behavior from the social customer is causing chaos to companies big and small, and forcing them to adapt their business models.

There's perhaps no better native and out-of-the-box use for social media in business than for customer support. The social customer is online and increasingly bound to social media networks of all types. A 2009 study by Cone Research revealed that 43 percent of consumers expect companies to use social networks to solve consumers' problems. It's no surprise, then, that these same customers also assign enormous convenience value to resolving the inevitable customer support problem via their favorite social network.

Companies can integrate customer support initiatives with social media in two ways. The first is to assign social media practitioners to data-mine the Internet looking for customer support-related inquiries that they can respond to. This can be achieved easily by investing in social media listening software and monitoring brand- or product-related terms (see Chapter 2, "Surveying Technology Supermarket," for more information on social media listening software). The social media practitioners can then either fix the issues themselves or create processes and workflows to filter and assign the identified conversations to the appropriate support channel. Second, and probably a better long-term solution, is for organizations to operationalize the support department to include social media as a viable support and outreach channel, just as they would a contact form on the corporate website or a toll-free number. Many companies today are doing both.

Due to Twitter's real-time conversation, it's natural for social media practitioners to use this channel to address customer issues. However, some companies are also monitoring comments on their YouTube channel and Facebook Wall, and within the corporate blog. They're also watching for comments posted on third-party sites, such as their competitors' pages and Amazon.com's review pages.

Companies have taken a variety of approaches to integrating their customer service efforts with social media. Many of these companies are being proactive and thinking long term about addressing the social customer, but others have been thrown directly into the fire.

Comcast

In spring 2008, Michael Arrington, founder and co-editor of TechCrunch, a blog covering the Silicon Valley technology start-up community, wrote a blog post about his discontent with Comcast, a local cable service provider. After a cable outage, Arrington contacted customer support and had a horrible experience. Not only did Arrington write a blog post about his experience, but he also expressed his unhappiness multiple times on Twitter, which was retweeted several times.

This incident got a lot of press, and the conversation surrounding Comcast's poor customer service began to appear more often in multiple social channels.

Comcast responded quickly and set up the Comcast customer support Twitter profile and business initiative known as @ComcastCares, now used to solve customer problems on Twitter.

What's important to note here is that this one incident caused a significant culture change at Comcast and forced it to operationalize customer support around a new channel—in this case, Twitter.

Today Comcast is considered one of the leaders in customer support online and is often cited in case studies, blog posts, and whitepapers as a company that's using social media the right way. And, while Comcast still isn't perfect and still criticized, it is surely one company that takes social customers seriously.

Best Buy Twelpforce

In 2009, consumer electronics giant Best Buy empowered hundreds of retail employees to manage online customer support inquiries and company promotions using Twitter. Best Buy even used online media and television commercials to promote this initiative and educate its customer base. The way it works is pretty simple. Employees register their personal Twitter accounts on a Best Buy site called Best Connect. When registered, employees from across the company can send tweets from the @Twelpforce profile; they add the hash-tag #twelpforce to make their messages automatically show up under the twelpforce Twitter profile, with a credit to their proper Twitter account (as in "via @ mytwitterhandle").

The following pledge from Best Buy management to its employees sums up the company's intentions with this initiative:

> Why would customers want to talk to you on Twitter? The promise we're making starting in July is that you'll know all that we know as fast as we know it. That's an enormous promise. That means that customers will be able to ask us about the decisions they're trying to make, the products they're using, and look for the customer support that only we can give. And with Twitter, we can do that fast, with lots of opinions so they can make a decision after weighing all the input. It also lets others learn from it as they see our conversations unfold.

Best Buy is one of the first companies to publicly communicate that it is using Twitter to engage with customers. While some may consider this to be a bold move and hard to scale, this initiative certainly positions Best Buy as a company that trusts its employees and understand the importance of personal communication.

Of course, no company can guarantee that it will solve every support issue that arises online. But Best Buy's Twelpforce has taken the steps necessary to make an impact in solving customer problems.

Zappos

Tony Hsieh is the CEO and founder of Zappos.com, an online shoe and retailer store that Amazon acquired in 2009 for $1.2 billion. Today nearly one-third of all Zappos employees are using Twitter to solve customer problems. What's important to note here is that this shift in culture dynamics started at the top, with Hsieh himself engaging with customers in social media. What was once chaos trying to manage customer support online is now standard operating procedure. The social customer is top-of-mind for Hsieh, Zappos, and several hundred employees who use Twitter. The reputation of Zappos customer service has been amplified through normal conversations on Twitter. These conversations aren't meant to drive up sales or even offer promotions. They're simply meant to please and educate the social customer, either new or existing. Such external engagement has also resulted in cost-savings. According to tech blog ZDNet, Zappos estimates the cost of reaching out to past, present, or potential customers on Twitter at $300,000 a year.

Additionally, one of the company's core values is to deliver "WOW" through service. All new employees are required to undergo a four-week customer loyalty training course, which includes at least two weeks of talking on the phone with live customers in the call center. After the training is complete, employees are offered $3,000 to leave the company immediately, no strings attached. This ensures that employees are there for the love of the job and passion for customers; not the money.

Zappos has created a culture of service and empowers each employee to join Twitter and delight customers. The company's culture focuses on making sure every possible interaction with customers results in them saying, "WOW, that was the best customer service I've ever had." And the initiative seems to be working: Zappos has seen triple-digit revenue growth over the last three years.

These examples have shown the evolution of companies using Twitter to solve customer support issues. They also have tremendous opportunity to use the collective intellect of the community to innovate their products.

Using Social Media to Solicit Product Feedback and Innovation

Some forward-thinking companies have already started listening to customer feedback on social media channels and are innovating their products, services, and business processes. This is also known as crowd sourcing. A company uses the collective intellect of the community to create or co-create a product or initiative. As a result of involving social customers in the decision-making process, the company fosters customer and brand advocacy and encourages loyalty to the brand. Companies such as Dell, Starbucks, and Microsoft have established such programs and are seeing a tremendous impact on the level of engagement with the community. In some cases, these companies are improving the customer experience for millions of customers and solving real business problems at the same time.

Dell IdeaStorm

Dell launched IdeaStorm in February 2007 as a way for the company to talk directly to its customers. The site allows Dell customers to view ideas posted by other community members, post new ideas about Dell's products or services, promote or demote ideas, and then see what ideas were actually implemented. In the three years since the site first launched, Dell has received more than 10,000 suggestions and implemented nearly 400 ideas. What's important to note here is that teams of Dell product managers spend time interacting with community members, sourcing good ideas that didn't necessarily make it to the top, and gaining insights into its customers' biggest concerns. The difference between Dell's program and what other companies are doing is that Dell is actually changing the way it does business based on community feedback.

Originally, the most popular suggestions concerned the Linux operating system on Dell machines. On May 24, 2007, just three short months after the site launched, Dell started selling three computer systems with Linux Ubuntu 7.04 preinstalled in the computers. The article requesting Linux eventually moved down the list and was replaced by newer ideas promoted by other community members.

MyStarbucksIdea

MyStarbucksIdea was built with the same intentions as Dell's IdeaStorm: to crowdsource ideas with the community. Community members can share, vote on, and discuss ideas, as well as see what ideas are being implemented. As with Dell, the entire community site is flooded with Starbucks employees listening to and engaging with customers. The site can be characterized as a real-time, always operating customer focus group. Since March 2008, the community has submitted more than 70,000 ideas.

A few suggestions that Starbucks has implemented include free coffee for Gold Card Members on their birthdays, a Starbucks VIP card, the infamous Starbucks Splashstick, and the program that gives customers a free cup of coffee when they buy coffee beans.

Intel's Ajay Bhatt T-Shirts

On a much smaller scale than the two previous examples, Intel took an idea one step further to delight its customers.

In 2009, Intel launched Sponsors of Tomorrow, a marketing campaign that centered on the people who work for the company, in an attempt to humanize the brand. Part of the campaign was a TV commercial titled "Your Rockstars aren't like our Rockstars." It featured Ajay Bhatt, Intel Fellow and the co-founder of the Universal Serial Bus (USB).

In the commercial, while Bhatt (played by an actor) is walking though the office, someone appears in the back holding open a T-shirt with Bhatt's face on it. The commercial was uploaded to YouTube and shared across the Internet on various web properties and blogs; then it was amplified through Twitter. Within days, these communities were begging for Ajay Bhatt t-shirts. They were tweeting about it, commenting on the Intel blogs, and posting on the YouTube channel and in third-party tech blogs.

Intel moved fast, printing 100 Bhatt T-shirts and giving them away as part of a month-long contest on Twitter. After the T-shirts were shipped, the winners began to post pictures of themselves wearing the T-shirts to Twitpic and Ajay Bhatt's Facebook Fan Page.

These three companies have more in common than just the fact that they're listening to social customers. They were also cited in a 2009 case study by Charlene Li and Wetpaint titled *Deep Brand Engagement Correlates with Financial Performance*. The report examined the top 50 brands and measured their depth of engagement with consumers on the web; it also looked at their financial performance for the last 12 months. The analysis showed that the companies that were more engaged in social media were seeing an increase of around 18 percent in revenue during the reporting period; companies that were least engaged suffered an average of 6 percent decline in revenue. Dell, Starbucks, and Intel were all listed among the top 10 companies in social media. It's not an exact science, but it's good food-for-thought for brands that are seriously considering social media engagement.

Taking the Next Step

The first step in addressing social customers is to decide who internally will be interacting with them. Someone in customer support? The CEO? A dedicated community manager or a social media practitioner who spends his or her days sourcing brand-related conversations and participating when appropriate? In any of these scenarios, it's important that companies be ready to scale and grow. Why? Because once there's even an ounce of interaction between a company and the social customer, customers will expect the company to stay engaged all the time.

Companies need to think about ways to train social customers so they don't use Twitter just as a bullhorn every time something goes wrong. Setting up a support community similar to what Research In Motion has done is a great model to follow. RIM uses its @BlackBerryHelp Twitter profile for customer support, offering up tips and tricks and also linking to relevant BlackBerry.com blog posts and forum discussion threads.

> Companies need to think about ways to train social customers so they don't use Twitter just as a bullhorn every time something goes wrong.

One of the worst things any company can do is create a thriving community and then abandon it. Unfortunately, this happens all too often. Before launching new communities, Facebook fan pages, and Twitter profiles, a company must get a firm commitment from everyone involved to continuously engage in these channels. Otherwise, the company will surely be at the center of criticism and will probably be featured in a *Harvard Business Review* case study titled "What Not to Do in Social Media."

The next step is to get the customer support department involved, if it isn't already. In some cases, a company might need to justify human capital and overhead expenditures for any external engagements. Of course, the advantages of customer support engaging with the social customer goes far beyond where the audience is: Considerable cost-saving side effects can be had by augmenting service and support operations to include increasingly more social touchpoints and efficiency. According to research data from the help desk industry, the cost to answer a support call is between $13 and $40. Imagine a call center that receives an average of 1,000 calls in a 24-hour time period. On the lower end of $13 per call, that's $13,000 a day ($4.7 million annually), and this doesn't even take into consideration the cost-per-minute charges and other overhead costs to manage a call center.

Finally, it's important to note that crowdsourcing has grown since 2004 with the publication of *Wisdom of Crowds,* by James Surowiecki. In his book, Surowiecki argued that large groups exhibit more intelligence than smaller groups and that the collective intelligence of a community can shape business more effectively. That said, it's important for companies to create a community for their customers to interact in and make product-related recommendations. With services such as Get Satisfaction, companies can instantly create crowdsourcing and support related communities that are integrated with corporate websites almost instantly.

Social customers are here to stay and are gaining influence every day. They're not shy about providing public feedback about the companies and brands they use, either. This can be either a serious threat to a company or an opportunity to create customer advocacy. Companies need to keep the social customer top-of-mind when optimizing internal business processes and creating external engagement strategies.

In Response to the Social Customer: Social CRM

5

The global rise of social media usage has presented a huge opportunity for companies that want to acquire new customers and retain existing ones. With the amplified voice and influence of the social customer, it's much easier today for companies to identify these prospects and customers and determine their needs and concerns. This is certainly an improvement from when most firms were using traditional CRM systems to manage their sales and customer life cycles.

Customer relationship management (CRM) is a business strategy for managing a company's relationship with customers and prospects. It involves using technology to manage and synchronize business processes for sales, marketing, customer service, and technical support. The underlying goal of CRM is to find, attract, and win over new customers; retain current customers; and potentially reduce costs for marketing and client management. Social CRM simply adds social to the definition.

Social CRM is also a business strategy. It's one component that helps organizations evolve into a fully operational social business. It's a strategic business initiative that not only considers the social customer, but also requires collaboration, customized internal processes, and technology integration. With a successful social CRM initiative, organizations will know what to say to their customers and prospects, how to say it, where to say it, and when to say it, to provide a more relevant customer interaction.

Although the management of social CRM focuses internally on people, process, and technology, it is in direct response to the external social customer. Social customers use a variety of channels to express satisfaction or discontent about a product or service, so it's imperative that companies not only monitor these channels, but also be prepared to take action there. Additionally, prospects are simply social customers of other companies, so an effective social CRM program will equip sales teams to engage with them at the right time.

However, before a company can fully accomplish any social CRM initiative, it must ensure that it is capable internally first, which speaks to the entire premise of this book: *Before a company can successfully manage external conversations, it needs to master its internal conversations first.* This is especially important when a company wants to get its IT, customer support, sales, and marketing teams to agree to work together to address the many facets of CRM.

> Before a company can successfully manage external conversations, it needs to master its internal conversations first.

Social CRM is still relatively undefined, despite all the attention it's getting in the blogosphere. For now, put aside what the pundits are saying, along with all the terminology, jargon, and abbreviations. The following key facts will help bring some perspective on the growing nature of social media.

- By the end of 2010, more than 60 percent of Fortune 1000 companies will have some form of online community deployed for CRM purposes (Gartner Group, *Business Impact of Social Computing on CRM*)

- Member communities reach more Internet users (66.8 percent) than email, which is a traditional component of CRM (65.1 percent; Nielsen, *Global Faces on Networked Places*)

Many industry experts have different points of views on social CRM and how it's defined. This is because the social and technology landscape is moving so quickly that it's still being developed. It's important, however, to highlight these differences and showcase their perspective, to provide a more clear and well-rounded definition.

Various Definitions of Social CRM

Martin Walsh, who leads digital marketing at IBM, wrote that social CRM is a process of monitoring, engaging with, and managing conversations and relationships with existing and prospective customers and influencers across the Internet, social networks, and digital channels.

Paul Greenberg, author of the best-selling book *CRM at the Speed of Light: Essential Customer Strategies for the 21st Century* and also president of The 56 Group, LLC, says that social CRM is a philosophy and a business strategy supported by a technology platform, business rules, workflow, processes, and social characteristics that's designed to engage the customer in a collaborative conversation to provide mutually beneficial value in a trusted and transparent business environment. It's the company's programmatic response to the customer's control of the conversation.

Michael Fauschette, who leads IDC's Software Business Solutions Group, defines social CRM as the tools and processes that encourage better, more effective customer interaction and leverage the collective intelligence of the broader customer community, with the intended result of increasing intimacy between an organization and its prospects and customers. The goal is to make the relationship with the customer more intimate and tie it to the company by building a public ecosystem to better understand what customers want and how they interact with the various company touchpoints, such as sales and customer service.

Jacob Morgan, founder of Chess Media Group and social CRM expert, states that organizations have the same customer-facing problems today that they did last year, five years ago, and ten years ago. Social CRM is a strategic approach (supported by technology) that helps organizations solve these same customer-facing business problems, but in the context of how people's behaviors (who they trust, what they expect from brands, how they show, where they shop, and so on) and communication methods (social channels or Web 2.0, but traditional channels such as email, phone, and in-person discussions still apply here) have changed. Social CRM is an evolutionary business approach for solving customer problems.

What's important to extract from these definitions is that the core focus of any social CRM initiative is the external nature and influence of the social customer. It's equally important to establish a scalable technology infrastructure and organizational processes to serve as the foundation of the program internally. Of course, defining social CRM is much easier than deploying a full scale social CRM initiative within an organization. The following sections will serve as a guide to get started.

The Social CRM Response Process and Workflow

Imagine all employees in the company, regardless of what department they work in, equipped with a dashboard on their computer monitor. This dashboard includes all relevant and verified customer data, including recent purchase history, demographics, previous interactions, call support history, and recent tweets and Facebook status updates. Social media practitioners and support agents can use this data to provide a more relevant customer interaction via the social web, over the phone, and even in person.

To make this a reality, there must be a process that guides employees' decision on whether or not to take action.

Jacob Morgan, social CRM expert at Chess Media Group, describes this as the ARM process: a five-step process that revolves around action, reaction, and management. It's a response framework by which all customer interactions can be managed, evaluated, and responded to (or not responded to).

The first component of the ARM process requires an employee to identify, document, and track the conversations people are having online about the company's brand or products. The conversations may come from existing customers (satisfied or not), prospects, influencers, advocates, and even partners or vendors. The key to managing these conversations is to look for keywords such as *purchase, buy, bought, renewal, cancel, canceling,* or *cancellation* coupled with a brand/product, such as "I just bought this new Dell Laptop and I love it!" or "I am thinking about canceling my Netflix account."

The second component of the ARM process examines where the conversation physically happened. This can include the obvious channels of the social web, such as Twitter, Facebook, LinkedIn, blogs, YouTube videos and comments, and review sites such as CNET. It can also take place via the traditional lines of communication, such as a toll-free number, an online form from a customer support website, or even word of mouth. What's important about this component is that if the interaction is on Twitter, that the response must also be on Twitter (as in, "@madcustomer just saw your note about your computer. Please DM me with your email address so we can solve your problem"). Same goes for the other networks as well. The way a company responds might also vary depending on which community the customer interaction is taking place and the technology capabilities within that network.

The third component of the ARM process involves analyzing the sentiment of the conversation (probably the most difficult step) and then deciding whether any action needs to be taken. Technology vendors such as Lithium include a pretty accurate sentiment-analysis tool in their social listening software solution. Analyzing sentiment (or intent) is much easier to do during a live phone conversation because it's easy to determine whether a customer is happy, mad, or neutral based on the words they say and the tone of their voice. This is the one step in the process that will never be automated and requires some level of human intelligence. What's important to extract from these conversations is whether any action is needed.

The fourth element of the ARM process is to reconcile the current data, if any, about the customer with the external conversations that are being tracked. This is where the core customer data set (such as sales/support history or demographics) is taken from traditional CRM applications such as Oracle (Siebel), Sugar CRM, Pivotal, and Salesforce and integrated with external data (from sites like LinkedIn, Twitter, and Facebook) to get a more complete view of the social customer. Integrated social media data with traditional CRM data can answer important questions such as these:

- What was the customer's latest purchase, or what version of the product does he have?

- When was the last time the customer called into customer support, and was there a resolution?

- Is this a lead, a prospect, or a current customer? Where is he in the sales cycle?

- Where does the customer live, what is his annual income, and what is his ethnicity and other demographic data?

- What social properties does the customer belong to, and which is he most active in?

- How many friends does the customer have, and how influential they are?

The fifth component of the ARM process is to establish business rules. Every company is different and applies different intelligence to this process. One example is a series of consumer behaviors that triggers a set of actions—for example, a customer who just bought product A and registers it on the corporate website might trigger an email inviting her to be a part of an internal community. Business rules are not static and constantly change as both the internal business changes and the external customer evolves. Examples of business rules are a flag or trigger to a customer support or sales agent if a community member unsubscribes to a piece of content or a notification to sales when someone downloads a whitepaper of the latest product and asks to be notified to get more information.

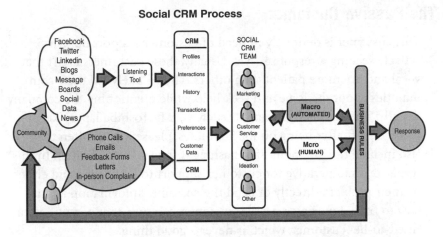

Figure 5.1   *The social CRM process takes into consideration the social customer and relevant profile data, such as previous purchase history and demographics.*

Applications of Social CRM

Social CRM can be used effectively to engage with several types of customers and prospects.

> Social CRM can be used effectively to engage with several types of customers and prospects.

The Venting Customer

This customer might be complaining on Twitter or Facebook, but a response might not be necessary. In many cases, these customers are just seeking attention from their networks and usually make statements such as, "I love my Dell laptop, but it's way too heavy," or "I just got Comcast installed. The high definition is amazing, but the cable box doesn't match my furniture, ugh." In certain cases, a company can choose to follow this customer on Twitter if that's where the conversation is happening and may even take it one step further and say "Thank you for ordering," or something similar.

The Passive Customer

This customer is definitely in need of customer support but isn't actively seeking a response—yet. Usually, these customers aren't that vocal and are more patient than others. They'll likely tell their communities about the issue and seek help while mentioning the company directly. They'll make statements such as, "My Toshiba laptop keeps powering off after being on for 5 minutes, please help!" Often they also include the infamous #fail hashtag if they're using Twitter. In this scenario, it's imperative for customer support to be flagged and either fix their problem directly or send the customer information about how to fix it. Ignoring a passive customer can turn that person into a "used-to-be" customer, which is never a good thing.

The "Used-to-Be" Customer

This customer is mad and very vocal, and needs the company to address the issue as soon as possible. These customers have most likely expressed their discontent several times online and either haven't been responded to or haven't had their problem resolved. They're consistently telling others about their negative experiences. They make statements such as "My Internet just went down again. I am sick of @Comcast and canceling!" or "1-800 Flowers was late delivering my mom's flowers for her birthday. This is the second time. I am done with them forever!" In this case, the customer support teams should be flagged immediately so that they can proactively reach out and offer them a complimentary promotion of some sort.

The Collaborative Customer

This customer is happy with the product, service, or company. Often times, these customers will seek out venues for suggesting new products or enhancements to an existing product, much like Dell's IdeaStorm and MyStarbucksIdea. They make statements such as "I think El Pollo Loco should also serve baked chicken for people who want to eat healthy" and then cc: the company on Twitter (as in "cc: @ElPolloLocoInc"). This, way, they ensure that El Pollo Loco will be notified via their @mentions on Twitter. Although this isn't a customer support issue, customers like this should be flagged and paid special attention to because they could potentially be turned into advocates. In this case, a marketing or a community manager should be flagged, and the customer should be added to a list and leveraged for future product launches or promotions.

The Customer Advocate

This customer will talk about a brand, product, or service even if he or she is ignored. These customers don't need incentives, either. They talk about a product because they're thrilled with what it does for them and how it makes them feel. Often they make statements such as "You all should buy the new Sony 3D TV. It is awesome and perfect for gaming and watching movies on Blu Ray. We love it!" Marketing and PR departments should be flagged immediately and should reach out to these advocates. It's good practice to invite advocates to private communities and give them sneak peaks into future products, seeding them with new products or just asking them for specific feedback.

The Future Customer

This customer, also known as the prospect, is one of the reasons CRM systems came into existence. They can either be new customers or customers who are considering an upgrade to a new product or service. The prospect will say things such as, "I am thinking about getting Comcast. Tired of Dish Network's constant outages. What do you guys think?" What could be a future customer for Comcast is potentially a "used-to-be" customer for Dish Network, so each company would handle this scenario differently. In any case, the sales team from Comcast should be flagged immediately and should be prepared to offer this customer a really good deal for switching services. In a business-to-business (B2B) environment, this could be an existing customer talking about upgrading the hardware in the data center; the account manager should reach out to them directly before the competitors do.

Just as various types of customers in the social landscape require attention, companies that want to achieve social CRM effectiveness must vary their approaches. Before doing so, however, there needs to be alignment internally on the roles and responsibilities for all stakeholders involved in the social CRM process.

Social CRM Roles and Responsibilities

Any social CRM initiative needs key support from a variety of different job functions from within a company to succeed. Depending on the size, culture, and dynamics of the company, these might shift or be managed in unusual business units—for example, marketing might own the customer service function.

IT plays the most important role in the deployment of any social CRM initiative because it is the gatekeeper of all the internal technology resources. The IT team has access and information about the entire portfolio of web assets and IT infrastructure hosted internally or on the cloud. They also have insights into the current social CRM applications and technology capabilities that the company is currently deploying. IT plays an instrumental role in integrating the existing CRM application with other, external platforms such as Radian6. IT might even own and manage the contractual relationship with each vendor.

The sales team is also crucial in helping make the social CRM initiative a success. Its input on prospects, sales cycles, and current sales processes are key to integrating into new customer workflows. The sales team will likely have really good customer and CRM intelligence because most of their time is spent using CRM applications to acquire new customers and manage the existing sales lifecycle.

Customer support departments play an equally important role in social CRM. Their responsibilities include drafting workflows and processes to address customer inquiries externally. Much of their time will be spent working through the ARM process and interacting with the social customer through the CRM application. They'll also work closely with IT or the CRM vendor to supply inputs and requirements to their support dashboards.

The marketing and public relations departments will need to collaborate and either provide their specific recommendations on which vendors to use or supply existing information on which social vendors they're currently using (such as Sprinklr or Radian6) to engage externally with customers and for social listening. They also have to work closely with support teams and give input on external engagement processes with customers on Twitter, Facebook, and other social channels.

Many companies also have collaboration teams that serve as project managers and ensure support, collaboration, and communication across each of the functional teams. They might also be responsible for managing deadlines, following up with stakeholders, and even "owning" the social CRM initiative until it's fully deployed and operational.

Much of this chapter has been spent defining social CRM, establishing a process model, showcasing practical examples of social CRM in action, and discussing various roles and responsibilities in the organization. The next step is to research the social CRM vendors and understand the technology available for deployment.

A Look at Social CRM Vendors

A full-scale social CRM solution should include communities, collaboration, social analytics software, social media listening applications, and a traditional CRM platform. Chapter 2, "Surveying The Technology Supermarket," highlighted many of these vendors—such as Jive, Microsoft, IBM, Tibbr, Sprinklr, Radian6, and Lithium—whose software platforms are at the cutting edge of their respective categories.

It's no secret that the nature of business relationships is changing. The speed at which consumers and businesses can learn more about each other before ever having a face-to-face or telephone interaction is staggering. The following vendors were chosen because they're building tools to keep pace with this accelerated rate of change. Of course, few social CRM vendors offer a full, comprehensive solution, but some are well on their way and others are doing some new and innovative things.

SugarCRM

SugarCRM is an open-source software solution and traditional CRM vendor. SugarCRM provides packaged sales, marketing, and support tools in addition to a highly extensible platform. It also provides social features but enables users to decide how to leverage social data and channels inside the Sugar system. For example, users can quickly and easily monitor Twitter streams of contacts or accounts, as well as instantly uncover relationship capital from networks such as LinkedIn right inside the CRM record. Additionally, the Sugar platform enables users to embed photos, blogs, and other social data right inside the system at the dashboard or the record level.

In addition to offering a flexible take on social data, SugarCRM has layered next-generation collaboration capabilities into the Sugar product line. Sugar Feeds enable users to collaborate and share data in a more ad hoc manner than through traditional email. Sugar Feeds can also be set up to alert users and managers of important changes in the status of existing accounts, prospects, or customer support cases. Feeds can also house multimedia and other files, such as a YouTube video that might help users learn about the market or product they provide.

Although SugarCRM has built many social tools into its platform, the vendor also understands that many vendors are focused on social media in other interesting and valuable ways. Thus, SugarCRM also leverages partners to expand the social capabilities of its product. For example, integration with Qontext enhances Sugar Feeds so that users can fully interact with their customers inside the Sugar system, collaborating on such processes for support case resolution. This is a great advancement over other collaboration tools, which can be accessed only by internal employees and not actual customers. Also, a partnership with Box.net enables fast, simple sharing of documents between Sugar users and their customers. For example, a Sugar user could quickly invite and share a contract or invoice with a customer, all instantly visible and edited in real time right inside the Sugar user interface. SugarCRM also partners with sales intelligence providers such as InsideView, which enables sales and marketing professionals to gain valuable insight into their prospects and customers from social channels from around the Web in an automated fashion.

Pivotal Social CRM 6.0

In June 2010, CDC launched Pivotal Social CRM 6.0, a social product that integrates with its traditional CRM application. It also integrates with external social channels such as Twitter, Facebook, and LinkedIn. This solution equips companies to identify qualified leads, gather sales intelligence through increased collaboration with customers, develop effective sales campaigns, help close more deals, and improve customer service.

Pivotal Social CRM integrates external conversations into the native Pivotal CRM application. This social product is built specifically for Pivotal CRM 6 and integrates with the most popular and ubiquitous social media channels, including Facebook, LinkedIn, Twitter, InsideView, and Google BlogSearch. The goal of this integration is to gain insights and intelligence into customers' and prospects' daily activities via the social stream. This application also incorporates the social stream into daily workflows of the sales, marketing, and support teams.

Additionally, Pivotal Social CRM offers the capability to streamline all public communication messages into one view. It also enables companies to broadcast marketing messages to existing CRM contacts and external community within the database. This makes it easy to expand, grow, and cross-pollinate the various external communities by inviting customers, prospects, employees, and everyone else in the Pivotal CRM database to connect with each other and the company.

Within the applications, it's easy to identify prospects and find out what they're saying, who they're saying it to, and where they're saying it. Additionally, the applications allow companies to take immediate action within the CRM system, assigning tasks to other stakeholders and follow-up as appropriate. Monitoring social media conversations and updates from the social stream can help sales teams uncover potential revenue opportunities and provide intelligence about the social customer.

It's just as easy to monitor customer support-related questions as it is to monitor sales conversations. Pivotal Social CRM enables companies to get a pulse on what is happening on external social media sites for reports of customer issues, complaints, or questions about products and services. Its application enables support teams to capture support incidents, create tickets, and assign them to internal stakeholders for resolution.

Pivotal Social CRM enables marketers to broadcast messages to all external social media channels in one click; this dramatically reduces the time and effort required to coordinate messages across multiple channels. It also goes one step further and enables companies to manage online and in-person events on Facebook from within the native application.

Nimble

Nimble's suite of products ranges from solutions for individuals to solutions that enable team collaboration, robust business reporting, automation, and forecasting. Nimble combines contact management, activity management, sales and marketing automation, traditional and social media communication tools, and collaboration features in one web-based solution. It imports, merges, and unifies the "3 Cs": contacts, calendars, and communication. It's easy to connect Nimble to any social network and unify all contacts. In addition, Nimble enables individuals to send and receive messages, status updates, and other social information. It also automatically searches social media sites, identifies relevant connections, and ranks them in relevance. After key information is identified, fully integrated collaboration tools enable individuals to share and act on that information among those who need it most to accelerate sales, marketing, and support processes. Nimble enables teams to more effectively communicate and collaborate via microblogging, which is tied to the customer record.

Any professional or business that works with end users and collaborates internally can use Nimble—in a social business, that's just about everyone. Depending on the size of the organization, just a few people might be using Nimble and performing multiple tasks. Entire departments and teams also can use Nimble for internal and cross-functional collaboration. For example, the group that always has a direct line of communication to customers is customer service. Using Nimble, support teams can easily listen for support-related opportunities, complaints, questions, and distressed customers in appropriate channels. They can immediately understand which customer record the service instance relates to, track the background of this customer's past multichannel communication history and past purchase behavior, and respond accordingly. Each response automatically logs as part of the customer record, keeping everyone on the same page both inside the service team and cross-functionally.

Marketing, public relations, and social media teams that are conducting influencer, analyst, and press outreach can use Nimble to track who has reached out to a particular person, as well as see the history and outcome of all communications. For sales teams, Nimble provides the same intelligence in researching key customers' and prospects' needs and responding to them accordingly. The sales organization can also use Nimble's opportunity identification and forecasting to increase prospecting and revenue. Marketing teams can use Nimble's connectivity to services such as MailChimp to understand the impact of email campaigns on customer and prospect activity.

Taking the Next Steps

Start small when creating a full-scale social CRM initiative. The biggest challenge is getting all the necessary players in one room and agreeing to actionable next steps. Collaboration is key, but having support from senior management will also help.

Several smaller-scale CRM efforts might already be happening throughout the company, so a significant amount of research and information gathering could be necessary. The information needed is who owns the company's CRM initiative, which current CRM application is being deployed, and whether that CRM system has any built-in social capabilities. It's also necessary to understand what social technologies the company is currently using (for example, social media listening software and collaboration applications), as well as which external communities the company is involved in (Twitter, Facebook, and branded communities). Strategic decisions will have to be made after all the CRM efforts are documented. The company will have to decide either to integrate all existing CRM deployments into a single cohesive initiative, abandon the programs that can't scale or integrate, or leave the situation as is.

Start small when creating a full-scale social CRM initiative. The biggest challenge is getting all the necessary players in one room and agreeing to actionable next steps.

Finally, a vendor analysis or Request for Proposal (RFP) will be required to identify which social CRM solution will work most effectively for the company. It's important to make this decision wisely and ensure that all the key players are involved in the vendor-selection process. A social CRM vendor isn't one that can easily be switched, due to the complexities of technology integration. It will be a serious business concern if a company's existing CRM vendor doesn't have social integration on the product road map and lacks plans for opening an application programming interface (API). This will surely impact the progress of any social CRM initiative, and decisions will have to be made to address this.

Social CRM doesn't have a light switch that can just be turned on when a company decides it's important. It's a strategic business initiative that requires time, commitment, planning, effort, collaboration, technology integration, and a budget. It's a complete shift from the way companies are used to dealing with customers, so it demands organizational change and behavior across multiple teams and business units.

Regardless of what the right definition of social CRM is, it's a well-known fact that the social customer exists today. And although social CRM focuses internally on culture, process, and technology, it's simply in response to the evolution and influence of social customers and their behaviors on the Internet.

Establishing a Measurement Philosophy

6

A company can measure the success of its social media initiatives in a variety of different ways—based on sales; the quantity and growth of friends, fans, and followers; or the volume of online conversation about a specific product launch. In today's business environment, marketing teams don't have the time to look at multiple data points to determine the success of a program or initiative. Companies need to adopt a simple yet comprehensive measurement philosophy that's completely supported by internal stakeholders. The challenge is finding that "right" measurement philosophy that provides business value to the company.

Social media measurement metrics can be grouped into two high-level categories: those that have a financial impact and those that don't. Measurement metrics that have a financial impact on the business are referred to as return on investment (ROI) metrics. These metrics measure the amount of money invested on a program or initiative and the amount of money received from that same program or initiative. Creating a metrics model aligned with the purchase funnel also has a financial impact, specifically at the sales phase. The purchase funnel is a theoretical journey that customers go through before they purchase a product or service.

Measurement metrics that don't have a financial impact include general engagement metrics such as fan/follower growth, retweets, total "likes," shares, and comments, conversation volume, and so on. These metrics help the brand build a relationship with the consumer, which can ultimately lead to referrals and long-term sustainability for the brand. In addition, web metrics such as unique visitors, page views, and time spent on a site are important to track and monitor to understand the levels of engagement users have with a company's web properties.

With so many possible data points to consider, companies need to avoid getting overloaded with too many metrics. Instead, classifying measurement metrics into meaningful groups will help streamline the measurement process. Additionally, when establishing a measurement strategy, it's always important to answer the question "What business problem does this solve?" to ensure that the measurement practices align with overall business objectives. Many companies today refer to this as key performance indicators or KPIs. This makes it much easier to quantify the value of measurement and to justify the cost by showing exactly what problems are being solved. The easiest example to illustrate this point is a company that wants to increase sales of a new product. The measurement philosophy

> When establishing a measurement strategy, it's always important to answer the question "What business problem does this solve?"

associated with this initiative must clearly include sales- or conversation-related metrics.

Choosing a Measurement Strategy That Works

Companies can categorize metrics in a variety of ways, depending on what makes the most sense for their business. What's important to understand is that all the metrics discussed in this chapter are generally the same; they're simply classified and reported differently.

The most sophisticated metrics modes include some level of financial impact, such as ROI. ROI plays a significant role in purchase funnel metrics and owned, earned, and paid media value.

Defining and Understanding ROI

According to a 2009 survey facilitated by social technology vendor Mzinga and Babson Executive Education, only 16 percent of the survey respondents said they currently measured ROI for their social media programs. In fact, more than 40 percent didn't even know whether they could track ROI from the tools they were using. This survey indicates that although many companies are adopting and using social media technologies within their organizations, they don't fully understand the true business value of these financial investments.

Ben Parr, co-editor of the popular social media publication Mashable, recently said that "the most effective enterprises in social media need to be relentless in tracking ROI. It's not just about tracking retweets and comments; it also means tracking click-through rates, customer acquisition metrics, and page views. There's a rapidly expanding market for tools that track these ROI metrics, especially as more businesses expand their social media operations. The technologies that will persevere will be the ones that track the most ROI metrics with the greatest accuracy."

And although many of the metrics listed in this chapter have no financial impact on the bottom line, it's important to discuss the ones that do, such as ROI. The standard formula for ROI is basic:

$$ROI = (X - Y) / Y$$

For example, if a company invests $20,000 and receives $100,000 in revenues, the ROI is (100,000 – 20,000 / 20,000) = 5 times the initial investment. Other, more complicated formulas take into consideration costs savings, such as a decrease in calls to a call center from launching a Twitter support channel. Understandably, ROI metrics are difficult to implement in the social landscape because community members don't want to be marketed and sold to. From a business perspective, however, a company needs a mechanism to track a consumer's intent to purchase or an actual purchase. One such mechanism is to develop a metrics model aligned with the purchase funnel.

Purchase Funnel Metrics

Purchase funnel metrics can do more than just track sales revenue. They can also give companies the capability to understand specific behaviors that consumers take when making purchase decisions.

The original purchase funnel was developed by E. St. Elmo Lewis, an American advertising visionary, in 1898. He proposed the AIDA model, which is an acronym for attention, interest, desire, and action. This model was derived from the belief that consumers go through a linear process in their minds when thinking about buying a product or service. Each stage depends on the success (or lack of success) of the previous stage, with the end result being a purchase.

New studies on consumer behavior, production saturation, and technology innovations, as well as the impact of social media, have changed marketers' thoughts on the purchase funnel. Many define it today as awareness, consideration or preference, purchase, and advocacy.

Each of these four metrics measures a different state in a customer's purchasing process.

Awareness

Awareness simply measures how aware a customer is of a particular product or service.

The most common of all awareness metrics is potential reach, which takes into consideration how many people (or eyeballs) a company reaches through its outbound communication messages. This includes any and all messages on Facebook, Twitter, and corporate blogs, plus the number of YouTube and Flickr views. Awareness metrics can answer the question, "Are people seeing our messages and do they know we exist??" Unfortunately, Facebook is the only site that gathers and reports on reach and impressions metrics. All other social channels require a manual count, unless a company invests in tools that can automate the process. Measuring reach in Facebook is relatively simple using its reporting dashboard, Facebook Insights. From this interface, marketers can pull reports and see how many fans are viewing the messages posted on the company's fan page in a given reporting period.

Twitter doesn't provide a tool for measuring reach, but companies can calculate this easily using a basic formula. This formula takes into consideration the total number of followers of the company's Twitter account, all retweets, and the sum of the followers of those accounts who retweeted the message. For example, if company A has 1,000 followers and they send out four tweets per month, their potential reach for that month is 4,000. If one of the tweets gets retweeted 10 times and each account has 1,000 followers, the total potential reach is the following:

4 tweets × 1,000 followers = 4,000, + 10 retweets × 1,000 followers = 10,000 equals 14,000 potential reach or impressions

Twitter reach can be easily measured using a tool such as Rowfeeder. Its platform automates all the calculations and exports all the data into an Excel Spreadsheet.

Summing the total views in YouTube, Flickr, or any other video- or photo-sharing site can be done by logging into the account page and summing the views manually.

Measuring reach for corporate blogs or communities requires summing the total number of RSS subscribers and total page views for published posts for that reporting period.

Many tools help in gathering all these metrics. One of the most sophisticated platforms is Sprinklr, also mentioned in Chapter 2, "Surveying the Technology Supermarket." This tool can pull data from any social media channel a company is publishing content to, including Facebook, Twitter, YouTube, and blogs. If an executive wants to see the total *potential* reach of all communications in a given month, Sprinklr can calculate all the metrics and provide one aggregated number. Rowfeeder is another tool that can pull data from Twitter and Facebook and report on reach metrics. Basic web analytics tools such as Omniture or Google Analytics can also gather data on page views and unique visits to a website or blog.

Consideration and Preference

Consideration and preference are combined in this analysis because it's difficult to determine what consumers are feeling unless they say so. This would require a complete "human" sentiment analysis, which isn't possible in some organizations unless they have a dedicated person who can assign sentiment to every social interaction with the brand. This isn't a scalable solution in many organizations.

That said, companies need to consider some basic assumptions when examining this portion of the purchase funnel. That is, if consumers are considering or prefer a certain brand or product, they're actually going to engage with it in some way. These are often referred to as engagement metrics, which can be measured for each social media site. Consider the following:

- **Facebook**—Fan growth, total likes, comments, views, shares, user-generated content
- **Twitter**—Follower growth, total lists, total retweets, mentions
- **YouTube (or other photo- or video-sharing site)**— Comments, favorites, embeds, shares
- **Blog or community**—RSS subscriber growth; total comments; shares via social bookmarking sites such as Stumblupon, Digg, or Reddit; listeners to a live chat; downloads of a whitepaper; content rating
- **Web analytics**—Return visitors, time spent on the site, page views per post, click-throughs to the corporate site from blog- or URL-tracking services such as Bit.ly

Another engagement metric for tracking consideration and preference is inbound links. In the most simplistic terms, an inbound link is a link from an external website or blog to a company's website or blog. The only caveat in this scenario is the actual context of the link. The blog post could very well be a complaint about the company's product or services.

Purchase

Purchase metrics simply measure what customers are buying. This is the strongest of the financial impact metrics because it allows marketers to measure the ROI of campaigns or programs. Unless a company is selling products directly from its social channels, this is hard to measure. The most straightforward tactic for measuring sales is to use tracking codes (or cookies) in links that are shared in the social landscape. The tracking code is embedded in a user's browser and reports on whether it resulted in a sale. However, some consumers don't like cookies, block them on their browsers, or frequently delete them which results in a loss of tracking.

Not all companies can use social media to sell directly to their customers, especially those in the business-to-business (B2B) space. Companies thus have to make assumptions to track these specific data points.

Many companies today must assume that if a consumer clicks a "where to buy" link, that person is going to buy the product. For example, Intel doesn't sell its processors directly. However, throughout the corporate website, Intel links to an online store, which is an API from CNET.com that pulls in feeds of computers with Intel processors. The transactions are managed and hosted directly on CNET.com.

Advocacy

An advocate is a customer who talks about a product, service, or brand without being asked to. These customers may or may not be influential in social media, but that doesn't stop them from talking about the brand and telling others about it.

The best way to track advocacy metrics is to proactively monitor conversations about the brand and engage with potential advocates. It also helps to develop a formal advocacy program.

A formal advocacy program can measure this portion of the purchase funnel in several ways, including these:

- How often the advocate is sharing branded content or product reviews

- Month-to-month growth in an opt-in advocacy program

- Participation metrics in a user community

- Number of attendees of a round-table discussion group

- Frequency and sentiment of positive conversations usually revolving around a recommendation of a product within Facebook and Twitter

- Redemption rate of coupons, discounts, or offers shared within the community

Social platforms such as Zuberance allow companies to create targeted advocacy programs and can measure many of the data points just listed. And although it can be an expensive endeavor to create a formal program, it's important to understand that advocates play an integral role in a company's marketing strategies, so it's an investment worth considering. Chapter 10, "The Rise of Customer Advocacy," goes into great detail about creating formal advocacy programs.

The purchase funnel is complicated, and every company can modify it to suit its unique needs. The metrics listed here help companies understand the purchase funnel and where in that funnel their customers and prospects lie. Most marketers aren't in a position to collect and manage every known metric, so it's important to focus on the ones that can be used as benchmarks and points of learning and that add value back to the business.

Another measurement philosophy that has financial impact is to measure paid, earned, and owned media value.

Paid, Earned, and Owned Media Value

Paid, earned, and owned media value is defined as the monetary value of impressions delivered from different marketing channels and assigning an equivalent cost per thousand impressions (CPM) that a company is willing to pay (or has paid) for those impressions. If applied correctly and strategically integrated into purchase funnel metrics, it can help companies prioritize their marketing spending and understand their returns in each of these channel investments.

The formal definition of paid media is a communications message from a company to consumers delivered by paying a channel (or website) that the company doesn't control. Examples of this are paid search, display advertising, and sponsored web content on a third-party website. Traditional media such as television and radio ads and out-of-home channels (billboards, cinema, and so on) also fall into this category.

Many companies today have slightly tweaked the purchase funnel to measure paid media initiatives:

- Awareness = Total ads served or impressions

- Consideration = Total users who clicked on an ad (a.k.a. the click-through rate)

- Preference = Number of users who engaged with branded content (watched a video, commented on a blog, subscribed to content, and so on)

- Purchase = Number of users who purchased a product or clicked on a "where to buy" link directing them to a retailer or partner site

- Advocacy = Number of users who joined a community (such as Facebook) or followed on Twitter

Owned media are messages delivered from a company to consumers through the company's own channels, such as a professional Facebook page, Twitter account, branded communities, or corporate website. Metrics associated with owned media include the following:

- Facebook = Impressions (traffic) and total reach generated through branded messages shared on the Facebook Wall

- Twitter = Total reach generated through tweets shared and retweeted by the community

- Internal/external communities = Total traffic (page views and visitors)

- YouTube (or other video- and photo-sharing sites) = Total video views

- Advocacy = Number of users who joined a community (such as Facebook) or followed on Twitter

Owned media value is the total monetary value of the impressions generated through marketing messages sent to the community and visits to owned media properties—and then assigning an equivalent CPM that a company is willing to pay for those same impressions.

Earned media is any message about a company that is shared between consumers as a result of an experience with the brand. Companies can look at earned media in two ways. In the first, a particular message is shared between consumers as a result of a specific experience with the brand, such as a positive experience with customer service or a new product one customer just purchased. In the second, a message is shared between consumers as a result of a deliberate social media marketing initiative. Examples of earned media can be any type of word-of-mouth marketing activity, viral programs, influencer outreach, and even formal customer advocacy programs. Metrics associated with earned media include these:

- Facebook = Comments, likes, shares on branded fan pages resulting in additional impressions through a friend's news feeds

- Twitter = Total retweets, @replies, and @mentions resulting in impressions to followers of the profiles tweeting a particular Twitter handle

- Internal/external communities and blogs = Comments, Facebook/Twitter shares, content added to social bookmarking sites

- YouTube = Comments and ratings
- Positive third-party blog posts, tweets, Facebook status updates, product reviews, videos, and all other user-generated content

Earned media value is the monetary value of consumer actions generated in social media channels that result from an interaction—and then assigning an equivalent CPM that a company is willing to pay for those impressions.

Community Health Metrics

Some organizations are less concerned with ROI and consider the health of the community to be a higher priority. The metrics associated with community health have no financial impact on the bottom line. Community health metrics can be classified into three different categories: growth, satisfaction, and engagement.

> Some organizations are less concerned with ROI and consider the health of the community to be a higher priority.

Community growth takes into consideration an increase or decrease in several factors:

- Community membership
- Content views and downloads
- Content or channel RSS subscriptions
- Comment-to-post ratio
- Unique visitors and page views

Acquisition metrics can also play an important role in community growth. If a company is using paid media to drive traffic to a community site, it's important to measure how many of the users who arrived at the community actually signed up and created a profile. For example, if a paid media program drove 1,000 users to a community site and 200 of the users created a profile, the conversion rate would be 20 percent.

Community satisfaction measures how pleased community members are with the company, the community platform, and the content shared within the community. Satisfaction metrics can include an increase or decrease in the following:

- Customer retention

- Customer satisfaction scores (CSAT)

- Customer loyalty scores

- Overall sentiment within the community

Community engagement, which most of this chapter covers, is the way the community members interact with each other and with the content. It includes increases or decreases in the following:

- Likes, shares, and comments

- Twitter @replies and @mentions

- YouTube comments and embeds

- Blog comments

Relevancy is an important factor when interacting with a community. If the content shared within a community is relevant, the metrics will certainly reflect growth and new members will join. Irrelevant content will result in a decrease in community health, and members will abandon the community to go elsewhere. Although there's no direct financial impact with community health metrics, they help gauge brand relevance across the social web.

Another way to measure brand relevance is to measure share of voice and sentiment.

Share of Voice and Conversational Sentiment

In some instances, a company or executive might want just the big picture. In this case, all that's important is whether conversations are happening about the brand online and how frequently those conversations are happening.

Share of voice is a company or product's conversational weight expressed as a percentage of a defined total market. For example, using tools such as Radian6, a brand manager for Adidas can measure the company's share of voice in the competitive landscape (such as, compared to Nike, Converse, and New Balance) to measure its share of the conversation among competitors in relation to shoes. This answers the question, "Are consumers talking about my product or my competitors' products?"

Companies can also measure their share of voice to use as a benchmark and track increases or decreases month to month to see if the volume of conversation is trending up or down.

Sentiment is the context of the conversations. It's usually categorized as positive, negative, or neutral. Even though sentiment isn't 100 percent accurate, it's an effective metric to gauge the overall tone of the conversation, monitor trends, and get a pulse on what's happening in the market. Most social media listening platforms include sentiment analysis in their core feature sets.

Measuring the Influence of Social Channels

Most companies have Facebook and Twitter profiles. Some of these profiles are influential and garner hundreds of comments, Facebook likes, and retweets, and are even cited by third-party media outlets. Other profiles are less influential and don't come close to achieving any level of engagement within their social channels. One way to measure how effectively companies are engaging in the community is to measure their own influence. Twitalyzer and Klout are the two leading social metrics platforms that can be used to achieve this.

Twitalyzer helps businesses large and small answer the question of "How can we measure the results of our time, effectiveness, impact, and investment on Twitter?" Twitalyzer offers more than two dozen metrics and measures, ranging from calculated metrics such as impact, engagement, generosity, and effective reach, to measures such as the number of updates, replies and references, follower and list counts, and how often an account has been retweeted. Some of the key metrics for measuring success include these:

- **Impact**—The number of unique references and citations of the user in Twitter, and the frequency with which the user is uniquely retweeted.

- **Engagement**—The ratio of people referenced by the Twitter user to the number of people referencing the user.

- **Effective reach**—This multiplies a user and each retweeting user's follower count by the user's calculated influence (the likelihood that the user will be retweeted or mentioned) to determine a likely and realistic representation of any user's reach in Twitter at any given time.

- **Tweet impressions**—Estimate of the exposure of a tweet, term, or hashtag used recently in Twitter.

Additionally, Twitalyzer has several reports that give companies a 360-degree view of their Twitter account from reports on metrics, goal setting, competitive tracking, tweet impressions, trending, and integration with Google Analytics and URL link shorteners (such as bit.ly, ow.ly, and others).

The second tool, Klout, measures a company's overall online influence. The Klout scores range from 1 to 100, with higher scores representing a wider and stronger sphere of influence. Klout uses more than 35 variables on Facebook and Twitter to measure true reach, amplification probability, and network score.

True reach is the size of an engaged audience and is based on followers and friends who actively listen and react to messages. Amplification score is the likelihood that those messages will generate actions (such as retweets, @messages, likes, and comments), on a scale of 1 to 100. Network score indicates the influence of the engaged audience, also on a scale of 1 to 100. The Klout score is highly correlated to clicks, comments, and retweets.

The final Klout score is a representation of how successfully a company engages its audience and how big of an impact its messages have on the community.

The Value of a Facebook Fan

In 2010, social media marketing firm Vitrue determined that the average value of a Facebook fan is about $3.60 in equivalent media each year.

The firm calculated this using a wide range of clients and their 45 million aggregate fans before arriving at the $3.60 annual valuation. A couple of assumptions Vitrue makes up front are that each status update posted by the company generates an average of one new impression for each fan. It also assumes that the brand is posting two updates per day. Finally, Vitrue placed a value on each impression by assigning a $5 CPM, which translates to $300,000 in earned media per month, or $3.6 million annually, for a fan page with 1 million fans. The mathematical equation follows:

1M impressions $\times$ 2 posts $\times$ 30 days = 60M impressions

60M impressions / 1,000 $\times$ $5 CPM $-$ $300,000

$300,000 $\times$ 12 months = $3.6M

$3.6M / 1M fans = $3.60

The one flaw in this equation is that the $3.60 valuation heavily relies on the fact that the company needs to post an average of 730 status updates a year to reach that $3.60 value per fan. That's just less than two posts per day, which is extremely high; sometimes overengagement can appear to be spam and can result in a loss of fans.

Additionally, the assumption of one impression per fan is a key metric to consider when calculating the earned media value discussed earlier in this chapter. However, equations like this must also consider the connectivity and influence of their fans and take into account key variables that include reach, frequency, and influence:

- **Reach**—Size or reach of a fan's personal network
- **Frequency**—Quantity or frequency of engagement
- **Influence**—Value of the actions a fan takes and the actions his or her networks take as a result

Assuming that the previous formula is right and all a fan does is consume content, a fan is worth $3.60. But what if a fan does more than just consume it? Wouldn't the value go up if she comments on it, shares it, and tweets about it? Wouldn't it also go up if his personal network has 1,000 friends instead of just 100 friends? This would be reflected in the number of impressions generated on the fan page, because the fans would inevitably drive more traffic if they were more influential and engaged themselves. All these factors need to be considered.

The point is that not all fans are created equal. Companies need to look at the number of impressions actually generated by Facebook posts and status updates. Then they must divide those impression metrics by the total number of fans to get a more accurate assumption of how many impressions each fan is generating.

Using the same formula, the following is a list of 10 high-profile brands and their calculated Facebook fan value as of January 2011:

- **Coca-Cola:** 96¢ cents (5.3M fans and posted 16 times in the last month)
- **YouTube:** $1.92 (4.8M fans and posted 32 times last month)
- **Pringles:** 30¢ (3.1M fans and posted 5 times last month)
- **Adidas:** $2.40 (2.7M fans and posted 40 times in the last month; also shares links to its e-commerce store, so we can assume that their fan value is much higher)
- **Red Bull:** $1.14 (2.5M fans and posted 19 times in the last month)
- **Starbucks:** $1.20 (6.8M fans and posted 20 times in the last month)
- **Pizza Hut:** $0.30 (1.2M fans and posted 5 times in the last month)
- **McDonald's:** $0.24 (2.1M fans and posted 4 times in the last month
- **NBA:** $8.22 (2.1M fans and posted 137 times in the last month)
- **Puma:** 84¢ (1.5M fans and posted 14 times in the last month

This formula isn't perfect, but it does give businesses that use Facebook insights into earned media value and the importance of posting relevant content that their fans will want to share. However, it also highlights some of the basic challenges of measurement.

The Challenges of Measurement

Numerous studies suggest that companies haven't yet fully attributed any business value to using social media. To this day, they're taking the shotgun approach to marketing because they don't know what's working and what's not.

In addition, it remains extremely difficult to attribute any social media activities to the bottom line. As much as this chapter highlights ROI metrics that map to the purchase funnel and earned media value, it's all based on assumptions, primarily what we think the customer is going to do next. The only exception is a company that's actively selling products through social channels.

Chris Brogan validates this point well in a blog post written in September 2010:

> A YouTube video with a million views has a bit more social proof than a video with 1,000 views, but beyond that, who cares? Did someone take an action based on the video? Did they type in the URL you flashed on the video? Did they follow through and do whatever you asked? The answer is almost always no.

In fact, this has been the challenge with all metrics models outside of direct marketing. Most experts in the industry would agree that social media does affect the bottom line (both positively and negatively), but no methodology or technology can be 100 percent certain. The argument to this, of course, is that social media isn't about selling, but is about building advocacy and long-term relationships with customers.

The last challenge with social media measurement is that there's no standardization of metrics. Social media can be measured in literally hundreds of ways. If 10 different marketers were asked how they measure social media, they would give 10 different answers. Even the marketing and PR team that works for the same company are probably measuring social media differently.

Taking the Next Steps

When establishing a social media measurement philosophy, it's important to ensure that all stakeholders actually agree with the approach. This includes what data will be collected, how often it will be reported, and what format it will be reported with. Success is determined by how much support is garnered by each stakeholder. It's recommended that social media teams reach out to internal counterparts early on and start thinking about standardizing metrics across the company.

It's also recommended to assign tiers to metrics and reporting. For example, a company that is measuring metrics at the purchase funnel and share of voice might assign that to tier 1; the data could be gathered once a week and sent to senior management for review. Social media teams could also present this data at a weekly task force meeting. Tier 2 metrics would be community growth or basic engagement metrics; reports would be generated monthly and be either sent to marketing teams via email or uploaded to a collaboration site. Tier 3 metrics could also be reported monthly and would encapsulate geography- or product-specific data. Ad hoc reporting would include measuring the influence of company social profiles and could also be used as a benchmark for daily, weekly, and monthly improvement.

> It's important to track and measure the effectiveness of the company's Twitter and Facebook profile.

Regardless of measurement philosophy, it's extremely important to track and measure the effectiveness of the company's Twitter and Facebook profile. Both Klout and Twitalyzer do this well. However, having an established process that determines which tool to use and how often to run the reports helps maximize community engagement and potentially the reach of marketing messages. More importantly, those who manage these accounts need to be prepared to act on the data. If the Klout score is showing a low amplification score, the account isn't getting many retweets; whoever owns the editorial calendar should then think more strategically about the content being shared so that it gets retweeted more often and translates into a higher Klout score.

It's easy to get overwhelmed by the wide range of tools and technologies that measure influence. Klout and Twitalyzer are two of many in the market today. OneForty.com, a social business software directory, is an online community for social media practitioners who want to discover the best tools to optimize their social media strategies. It's a helpful resource for enterprise marketers who are overwhelmed with the technology supermarket and on the hunt for measurement tools and applications for their business.

Finally, hiring a data analyst with experience in web metrics can be a smart move for any business that takes metrics seriously. An analyst with experience in paid media also can smooth the transition to social media because many of the same concepts and terminology apply. Proficiency in math and the ability to articulate data in a way that executives can understand it is also an important attribute.

So, if companies adopt the right measurement philosophy and measurement metrics, they can analyze the success of their social media initiatives.

7

How to Choose the Right Vendors, Agencies, and Technology Partners

For organizations trying to evolve into a social business, strategic thinking must be an integral part of operational procedures and the decision-making process. With social media's relatively newfound acceptance within business, minimizing barriers to success is critical. It is important to remember that perception is reality. The perception of any social media program, whether global or more focused (a product launch, events, a departmental initiative to connect with customers, and so on), has the potential to derail the program and buy-in for future social media initiatives.

Social media is still in the early days of acceptance as a meaningful and valued part of a company's communication mix and go-to-market plan. Proving this channel as relevant specific to a company, product, or brand and then evangelizing the success is critical for establishing long-term acceptance across the organization. Selecting a technology partner or agency is perhaps a topic not often associated with much strategic thinking. Often it is viewed simply as a digital or IT process: Vendors are interviewed, pitches are given, the members of a team discuss options, and then the decision is made.

For organizations trying to evolve into a social business, strategic thinking must be an integral part of operational procedures and the decision-making process.

This process warrants a much more strategic approach. Failure to match a vendor to the unique requirements of a business can cause a social media program to fail miserably, or worse, derail the momentum of a company's evolution into a social business. If the agency doesn't fully understand social media, it could make a misstep in execution. If a company doesn't understand the market and both how and why social media must be used effectively, its strategic moves could be all wrong.

Unfortunately, no one vendor offers end-to-end solutions that address all the social business needs of a company; so careful consideration should be used when choosing the right technology vendor.

Choosing the Right Technology Partner

Choosing a technology partner is the first step. Contrary to Forrester's POST Method (for people, objectives, strategy, and technologies), in which technologies are the last considerations, it's imperative to first identify the technologies needed internally, such as customer relationship management, collaboration software, and internal communities. Later in the process, after the company has adopted several social business initiatives, the company can hire external technology vendors

for community sites, social listening, and social relationship management as well as publishing platforms such as Sprinklr, the Syncapse
Platform, or Involver. Many times these technology vendors meet both
internal and external needs. For example, vendors like Jive have service
offerings that can support internal communities and collaboration
as well as external communities that can be used for customer
engagement.

Finding the right technology platform that can help operationalize
social media internally can be a tremendous task. The good news is
that dozens (several dozens, in some cases) of vendors are offering
"white label" solutions; the bad news is that this makes the process for
choosing one much more difficult. Additionally, many technology
companies are now consolidating, so in the near future, the number of
vendors may dramatically decrease. That being said, companies must
consider a few points when making this decision. In particular, companies must have a firm understanding of technology feature requirements, vendor support models, training, and maintenance, plus its
culture and leadership.

Several technology vendors (many are listed in Chapter 2, "Surveying
the Technology Supermarket") offer both community and collaboration feature sets. Many of them will also build social CRM functionality into their platforms. Most already have open APIs that integrate
with traditional CRM applications. The benefit of this is that companies can use one vendor for everything, which is cost effective and
easier to scale.

Understand the Organization, Culture, and Leadership

The choice of technology vendor must be a strategic decision.
Companies need to understand what they are trying to achieve before
thinking about which vendor to hire. Are they trying to streamline
communication between business units or geographies? Are they looking to roll out a collaboration application that will eventually replace
their intranet? Or are they planning to use social CRM and weave it
into their sales and marketing initiatives? Whatever the case, it's
important to understand the culture of the organization and its leadership. Social media will not change an organization's culture. However,
having a strong understanding of it will have a huge impact on the

technical requirements, choice of technology, and approach for implementing and configuring it.

When a company understands how the need for technology aligns with its own goals, it can start thinking about more tactical considerations, such as feature sets.

Understand the Internal Technology Suite

Some companies may choose not to hire agencies at all. Perhaps they have the internal staff and expertise to manage the planning, strategy and execution from beginning to end. In many cases, large organizations will facilitate all the planning, then define a strategy, and then hire an agency to execute. In smaller organizations, they may hire an agency to do everything. Much of this decision will depend on the level of social media proficiency and expertise that exist within the company. Because this is still a relatively new space, many companies need to hire an agency for strategic counseling, education, and guidance. For the more proficient companies, they may only hire an agency to execute a program, build a blog, or serve as community managers on Facebook and Twitter. Every company is different, so this decision will depend on the size, organizational model, and culture of each.

Before choosing any external technology partner, it's imperative to fully understand the company's existing internal infrastructure. Companies must answer several questions before making a decision:

- What current applications are powering the intranet or network?

- Can the existing network infrastructure support the technologies being considered?

- Is there enough network bandwidth to support the application? If not, how much will it cost to upgrade the network?

- Does IT have the resources (both human and technical) to support the integration and installation of the application?

- Can this solution be built in-house instead of being outsourced to a vendor?

The answers to many of these questions may change the direction of the plan, so it's important to understand what is and isn't possible within the internal landscape.

Technology Feature Sets

Companies need to choose technology vendors that do more than just provide the features and functionality needed in today's dynamic business environment. They must also choose vendors with features that might be needed in the future. For community-related software, some important features to consider include the following:

- Support for internal groups, forums, and profile creation
- Support for topical subgroups (private or open)
- Multiple-language support for global companies
- Support for microblogging, general blogging, group messaging, wikis, and chat
- Email support and integration
- Single sign-on (SSO) capabilities that integrate the platform with other internal registration databases, as well as external profiles such as Facebook and Twitter

Most of these features sets are standard among vendors, except for multilanguage support. For global organizations, this should be a must-have feature, especially if there are plans for global expansion.

Feature sets for collaboration software should include the following:

- Document sharing and control
- Task management, shared calendar
- Workflow-based and roles-based management
- Reporting analytics
- Self-service features that enable users to drag and drop of various widgets, to allow for customization of each user's interface
- Full set of APIs, for integration with third-party internal and external applications

What's important is that although many vendors have similar, if not exactly the same, features, much of the differentiation will involve price, scale, and customer support.

Support Models

Another consideration when choosing a technology partner is the support model. Many vendors today have their support teams overseas, in other parts of the world. No matter how good a software application is, support is sometimes necessary to troubleshoot a problem. Having a support team that is eight or nine hours ahead can potentially be disastrous.

Additionally, some technology providers may require a dedicated support staff per company or license, whereas others provide customer support for a fee. The cost of hiring support staff needs to be factored into the purchase decision. Support may come in the form of human help or an automated support engine. In some cases, there may be a need to have a dedicated support person on-site.

Before any decision is made, however, organizations should first conduct an audit of their existing IT vendors and analyze which support models work most effectively. Having a solid understanding of the suite of internal applications will help make the decision much easier.

Training

Training is another form of support and is imperative in helping an organization adopt and implement new technology. Some technology vendors offer free training (in person or via e-learning), to get companies up-to-speed quickly. In some cases, and depending on the size of the company, the vendor might offer paid training as well. This cost also needs to be factored into the purchase decision.

Determining the training needs of an organization may be difficult because most organizations take time to scale their effort and often expand in phases. That being said, planning beforehand will ensure that these questions are answered right from the start.

Maintenance Considerations

Maintenance models and cost-efficiencies have a major impact on the performance and adaptability of most technology vendors. When the application is hosted externally by the vendor, it's vital that the software be available and online at all times. This is referred to as uptime. In most cases, uptime expectations are covered contractually under the service-level agreement (SLA) and range from about 98 percent to 99.99 percent. Smart and innovative vendors are consistently improving their software applications, fixing bugs, and releasing new versions to existing customers at no charge.

For nonhosted applications, it's wise to get the IT groups involved early to ensure there is a common understanding of the existing infrastructure. Additionally, there will need to be internal support teams ready to manage, install, maintain and troubleshoot the application software.

When an organization has answered these questions and feels comfortable proceeding, it can start the process of hiring an agency.

Choosing the Right Social Media/Digital Agency

Selecting the right agency is a crucial business decision. Choosing wisely undoubtedly leads to positive marketing results, metrics that stand the test of time, return on investment (ROI), sales revenue, and, ultimately, long-term business value. On the other hand, making the wrong decision can have a reverse effect and most likely cost someone his job.

There is a new trend of "social business" agencies arising in the market today. The skill set of these agencies are different from that of social media marketing. They serve more as consultants and focus on change management, organizational models, governance, training and metrics. They are more strategic and often

Because this is still a relatively a new space, many companies need to hire an agency for strategic counseling, education, and guidance.

don't execute marketing related programs. Many consultants are also positioning themselves as "social business consultants" and have experience in working internally for large organizations.

In any case, the following is a systemic approach to agency selection: research, listen, act, and evaluate.

Research the Agency

Research is fundamental in agency selection. Developing a list of agencies is a first wise step before conducting research. Most business professionals have dealt with agencies in the past, so coming up with a list shouldn't be a difficult task. In many cases, compiling a list of referrals from colleagues should also be considered. Twitter is certainly a helpful tool for research. It's recommended that the list include four to six agencies.

Most of the initial research can easily be done on the Internet. Every agency today has a website that lists its service offerings, client roster, and company cultural tidbits, and the site often showcases bios from company leaders. It's important to determine whether the agency focuses on specific industry niches like network storage, food service, or packaged goods or has a broader focus like sports, entertainment, or technology. It's also important to research whether the agency's expertise aligns more with business-to-business (B2B) or business-to-consumer (B2C) initiatives. It's highly recommended to get the full client list from each agency, to ensure that a candidate doesn't already work with a direct competitor. Checking references early on will help weed out agencies that have questionable reputations.

A close examination of the list of services is also key. A few years ago, every agency (digital, PR, creative) started offering social media services simply by adding it to a website, pitch decks, and capabilities presentations. If an agency truly is a social media agency, examining the website closely should validate it. Are they blogging? Using Twitter? Does their content make any sense? Is their website optimized with social functionality with social bookmarks, Twitter, and Facebook? Simple observations such as these help narrow the focus and separate social media agencies from the ones who just add social media to a website as an add-on service. There is an important distinction between the two, because agencies that are socially proficient should be very active on Twitter, blogging, and also have some level of Facebook presence.

Finally, Google the agency name and study the results. This uncovers two important insights. The first is that it will show whether previous clients have publicly praised or criticized their work. Second, it proves how actively (or not) the agency is using social media to market itself. Investing in a conversational audit will provide more granular insight about the agency. A conversational audit uses tools like Radian6 and scours the web—such as blogs, Twitter, forums, news sites, and random web sites—for mentions of the agency name.

Listen to What They Are Saying

This step is the most critical. If the agency's leadership or employees are using Twitter or writing blog content, it's important to read the content of what they're sharing within their communities. This is crucial because an agency is a direct extension of the companies it represents. If an agency is using Twitter inappropriately, it may not be a wise decision to hire them. Examples of inappropriate behavior can include tweeting obscenities or sharing content about clients without any disclosure.

Additionally, it's important to listen to the agency's context or point of view about social media in general. If an agency believes social media should be more promotional than conversational, that candidate might or might not be a good fit. A few other considerations include these:

- Is the agency using the basic principles of disclosure and transparency?
- Is this agency using the latest technologies when executing social media programs?
- Is the agency providing any thought leadership in the industry, or is it simply recycling others' content?
- Is the agency strategic or merely tactical?

The key here is to get to know who these people are, what they believe, and how they interact within their own communities; listen to their online voices without them necessarily knowing.

Act Personally

After spending some time listening, a company's list of potential agencies might in fact shrink. Then it's time for a company to start the request for proposal (RFP) process. (Some companies call this a request for information, or RFI, instead.) The end goal is to collect some specific information from each agency on the list.

It's good practice to ask each agency if it is interested in participating in the RFP process. This allows any agency that doesn't want to participate to opt out of the process right away, saving everyone a lot of time and effort.

When developing the RFP, it's important to be as specific as possible about the requirements of the proposal. This includes company background, industry data, target audience, competitors, and the specific "ask" of the proposal. This ensures that the response is just as specific as the RFP.

Before sending the RFP to the participating agencies, it's good practice to ensure that all the internal stakeholders agree with the proposal, the on-boarding agency's proposed responsibilities, and the criteria for scoring them during the pitch. Nothing is more frustrating for an agency than to have to start the entire RFP process from scratch because someone on the internal team wasn't brought into the loop early.

Evaluate and Make a Decision

After receiving the RFP responses, it's time for a company to evaluate them. Common reasons for not making the cut are not following instructions, being late to return their proposal, or simply not being a good fit with the company's culture. When evaluating the responses, important questions to consider include these:

- Does the agency have enough social media experience?

- Does the agency understand the basic fundamentals of social media?

- Does the agency understand the business value of social media?

- Has the agency executed any social media programs in the past?

- Is this a metrics-driven agency?

- Is the agency too big? Too small?

- Is the agency creative or simply recycling old ideas?

- Does the agency have any thought leaders on staff?

Additionally, it's important to call references and specifically ask about the quality of work and overall satisfaction with the agency relationship. Some key areas to focus on include time management, deadlines, personalities, and synergies such as between the agency and client; also consider asking for a quick case study on a specific program that the agency executed.

Some companies require agencies to present their pitches, or capabilities presentations, more than once to different audiences within the company. It's important to explain this to the participating agencies up front. While the agency is presenting the proposals, evaluate the presenters' level of proficiency in presentation skills, their confidence, and team cohesion as well as how accurate they were with the task in the RFP. Of course, the most important criterion in evaluating the agency is whether there's chemistry between the company and the agency. This is probably one of the most important factors when making the hiring decision.

A Company Point of View to Agency Selection

This book wouldn't be complete if it didn't include some thoughts from decision makers working for fairly large organizations such as Adobe, Intel, and Cisco. One point to highlight is that choosing vendors or agencies is more than just one person's responsibility. It requires support, collaboration, and agreement from the broader organization to make the right decision for the business and everyone involved.

Maria Poveromo, director of social media at Adobe, says:

> When Adobe got organized internally around social media, we
> knew we needed an agency to help us build out our internal
> infrastructure (or center of excellence) while helping teams
> across the company to implement programs. We wanted an
> agency that could bring industry best practices, actionable learn-
> ings from other clients, and a combination of strong strategic
> counsel and implementation capabilities as we lacked the inter-
> nal resources to do everything ourselves. Also, we needed an
> agency that could understand our complex business and our very
> diverse audiences. But we also wanted an agency that we would
> partner with—one that would be a great fit and would comple-
> ment our team. At Adobe, we view our agencies and consultants
> as extensions of our internal teams, so finding the right agency
> partners is critical to the success of our programs.
>
> As my social media team was going to focus simultaneously on
> engaging with Adobe communities at a corporate level while
> organizing our hub and spoke model, we needed an agency
> whose skill set could span the gamut. The first thing we did was
> identify top agencies in the field and provide them with an
> overview of our business objectives and challenges. They were
> invited to present their recommendations. In order to ensure we
> used a consistent approach to our analysis of the participating
> agencies, we developed a score card that ranked the following
> criteria:
>
> - Social knowledge and expertise
>
> - Range of services (strategy consultation, implementation
>   capabilities, measurement, reporting, crisis management,
>   expertise in marketing communications and training)
>
> - Staffing (will their best employees be available to work on
>   the Adobe business?)
>
> - Ability to work with other agencies (Adobe, like many com-
>   panies, has other agencies of record—it is critical for the
>   social agency to be able to partner well with those)
>
> - Proven track record, ability to get results, case studies

- Quality of work (based on case studies and/or references)

- Size of agency (would we be a small fish in a big pond?)

- Cost (can they provide excellent work within the budget available?)

Kelly Feller, social media strategist at Intel, says:

So what are the qualities I look for when determining which agencies I might work with? The simple answer to that question is "It depends." At the highest level, I must ascertain whether the assistance I require falls into the "strategic" category or whether it's help with social activation that I need. I've found that the larger, more established agencies generally offer some excellent guidance when it comes to helping me formulate a social media strategy. However, I often look to smaller, local, boutique agencies when I need help activating social campaigns. Because these agencies often employ younger, more flexible social media practitioners who don't mind rolling up their sleeves and doing some of the activation work, it's natural that I look to them when I have campaigns that require things like travel in order to activate.

One of the critical items to consider when looking for an agency to help round out your team is the expertise of the individuals on your team. My current team, in particular, includes some of the smartest social strategists in the business. Because of this, we don't typically need as much strategic support as we do either creative thinking or assistance with activation. Finding an agency that possesses wildly creative ideas in addition to solid experience in the area of social media is truly the elusive holy grail of social media marketing. Oh, there are some out there, but they are few and far between, in my opinion.

Petra Neiger, corporate social media marketing strategist at Cisco, says:

I believe that agencies need to be able to provide business value to their clients. As a social agency, they need to be equally comfortable with strategy and execution. Sometimes they may be hired to help articulate a strategy, and sometimes they may be

tasked with execution, or both. They need to have a solid understanding of organic and paid search, earned and paid media, and
the target audience's online behaviors (not just offline). They
need to be able to look at holistically how these things affect each
other and make recommendations accordingly. They need to be
equipped to efficiently and effectively handle any potential
online crisis or other PR issues.

And last but not least, support is a critical consideration for practitioners. The best way to get to know an agency is in challenging
situations. Customer service is crucial. I believe this can be a
great differentiator in a space where there are hundreds, if not
thousands, of agencies offering similar services.

An Agency Point of View to Agency Selection

The company's perspective is certainly important to understand
because the company is essentially the "hiring manager" when it
comes to agency selection. At the same time, it's equally important to
understand the points of view from those who pitch big brands and
have been involved in many agency-client relationships in the past.
This section offers some powerful insights from leaders who work for
highly regarded social agencies, Ogilvy, WCG, and Ignite Social Media.

Rohit Bhargava, bestselling author of *Personality Not Included* and
executive vice president of strategy and marketing at Ogilvy, says:

When choosing the right agency partner, I'd say it comes down
to four critical factors: strategic vision, point of view, relevance of
experience, and depth of team. Strategic vision is first for a reason, because agencies make lots of money by delivering tactical
execution. They offer arms and legs for any marketing task, and
when they get fired, it is usually for lacking the strategic vision to
make all those tactical things they did actually matter. The second is a strong point of view and is usually the hardest to find.
The agencies that have this are the rare partners who will feel
okay disagreeing and offering a professional opinion. They are
the ones with the passion to care enough about your business to
really want to succeed. Often the difference between a great

agency and a mediocre one is that the great ones just have people who care more.

The third point on my list is relevance of experience, and this doesn't refer to only industry experience. Sometimes we get stuck in the trap of looking for only an agency that has lots of experience in an exact industry. If you sell data storage, it's tempting to go to the specialist group that already has done that. The problem is that they probably have another client (your competitor) that they have been used to working for and their best ideas are already spent. Instead, look for an agency that has experience in the *skills* that you are seeking, and you'll likely find much better thinking aligned to what you actually need them to do.

Aaron Strout, blogger and Head of Location Based Marketing at WCG, says:

> For me, I've always been fortunate to work with really smart people, many of whom either had written their own books or were often invited to speak at conferences. This form of thought leadership ends up being a great door opener to new business, mainly because it gives potential customers and partners an opportunity to look into the company's ideology when it comes to marketing, communication, and social medial.
>
> However, being able to articulate a thought process, having a point of view, and offering legitimate thought leadership is not enough to hire an agency. The real proof is in the actual work the agency has done for clients. Companies cannot settle for just logos on the agency's website. After all, hasn't everyone done a project with Kraft or Coca-Cola at some point in time? The real test should be real links to work that the agency or vendor in question has done. And the agency should be willing to connect you with the client (assuming you are serious about moving forward) for references.

Jim Tobin, president of Ignite Social Media, says:

> Most of the large legacy firms in PR, digital, and advertising are fighting to make their case why they should be in charge of your social media dollars. But the very strengths they bring to their

main disciplines often give them blind spots when it comes to social media marketing.

You need expertise on staff in search engine optimization, web development, blog outreach (which is very different than PR outreach), web copywriting, design, advertising, and much more. And you need a group conditioned to work across these disciplines in a fundamentally new way. When you're hiring, you want to look for the deep thinking in the proposals/examples that agencies show, not just the high level. Look for strong thinking around SEO, seeding strategies, and social spread. Also ask for the agency's blog. Take a look to ensure that it demonstrates thought leadership in social media marketing.

The key takeaway is that companies need to do their homework before hiring an agency. Ensuring that the agency is proficient in social media, community management, web development, copywriting, project management, and search engine optimization are key indicators of a good social media agency.

A Cisco Case Study on Vendor Selection

By keeping a close look on the external landscape, Cisco is positioning itself at the brink of innovation by using top vendors in the social space. After many individual one-off social media vendor discussions, in the fall of 2010, Cisco facilitated a comprehensive social media vendor sourcing event. This allowed Cisco to look at social media vendor management more holistically and strategically. Cisco brought in close to 30 different vendors from a variety of disciplines and asked them some very basic starter questions. To get started, each social media vendor candidate needed to submit a written RFI, and when Cisco felt there might be an opportunity for collaboration, the company invited the vendor to give a virtual presentation. Cisco had strict criteria, and several team members were a part of this vendor selection process. Starter questions included the following:

- Who are you as a company? Specifically, being a large corporation, we are interested in your ability to scale, whether you've have international experience, and your support and service model.

- What is your approach to social media?

- In your opinion, what do you believe is your key differentiator in this space? Why do you think it is important? In other words, why should we choose you?

- Show us who you are through real-life examples. What was the objective? What problems were you trying to solve? Or what opportunities were you trying to take advantage of? How did you go about it? What was the outcome?

Besides other members of the Corporate Social Media Marketing organization, feedback was solicited from the corporate social media communications team, the corporate events team, the corporate branding team, and the corporate media team, as well as a few selected practitioners in the business segments. The sourcing event was virtual and recorded, so any team member who was unable to attend the live event could provide input after each session. In addition, the social media team also reached out to social media teams from other, non-competitive companies to solicit feedback as well.

After the initial virtual presentation, Cisco then had to narrow down the vendor pool. When selecting individual vendors, Cisco considered the business needs and social strategy. These were categorized into five areas:

1. Social strategy development and consulting

2. Program or campaign development and execution

3. Tools and applications

4. Third-party paid social media and social media advertising and outreach

5. Social media platform provider

Cisco then shifted the focus to assessing the vendor's capabilities, both hard and soft skills. To Cisco, the vendor was just as important as the service model it came with. After several weeks of vendor meetings, the team selected a few vendors they had an immediate need for and granted them Cisco preferred vendor status. They also earmarked a number of other vendors they thought could offer some value to the company later.

The vendor sourcing event had several positive outcomes for Cisco. Not only did it help the corporation approach social media vendor management more holistically and strategically, but it also helped strengthen internal collaboration and streamline the process for future vendor engagement.

By keeping a close look on the external landscape, Cisco is positioning itself at the brink of innovation by using top vendors in the social space.

For companies evolving into a social business and ready to hire vendors to help them along the way, having a vendor fair is an excellent way to get a comprehensive view of the market.

> Having a vendor fair is an excellent way to get a comprehensive view of the market.

Taking the Next Step

Hiring a technology vendor and a social media agency can be critical to businesses. It can mean the difference between success and failure. Success equals strong partnerships, effective planning, and top-notch execution. More important are the results of the initiative. Great social media agencies deliver value; it's up to the company to decide what that value is, such as sales, community growth, engagement, or increasing share of voice.

Before jumping head first into finding the right technology partner, companies should listen, watch, understand, and interview the constituent base that will be using the technology internally. It's important to understand feedback and how the people and teams that will be using it will receive it. Additionally, ensure that there is high involvement and buy-in at the early stages of the initiative to establish collaboration and avoid internal pushback.

It's imperative to also initiate conversations with legal, human resources, and IT and privacy teams early, to understand the limitations and potential risks that may be associated with the technology initiative. As with any new business plan, companies need to do their due diligence and fully understand the risks involved with selecting, acquiring, integrating, and installing social technologies behind the firewall.

Companies also need to consider whether they should build or buy the technology they need. Many large companies do have the expertise internally to develop their own solution (such as with engineering and IT). They also have the infrastructure (server space, hosting, security, and applications) to support and maintain the development of robust internet/intranet applica-

> Great social media agencies deliver value; it's up to the company to decide what that value is, such as sales, community growth, engagement, or increasing share of voice.

tions. Companies often build their own applications instead of using an "off the shelf" solution because there is more control and the ability to customize is easier. However, the challenge in building the technology from scratch is timing and cost. Smaller companies will probably purchase solutions due to scale and lack of internal resources. All of these factors need to be considered before making any technology decisions.

In most companies, building a new social application can take years, mainly because most IT and network engineering teams are busy maintaining the company's network and ensuring that it's safe from intrusion. Unless the initiative is a business priority, a project such as this might take a year or two to even get started. In addition, ongoing support when something breaks can easily be a full-time job. It's important to determine early what the technology plan will be. If it's going to be built in-house, will there be enough internal resources to support the deployment and ongoing maintenance of the application? If purchased, is IT comfortable with the security of the application and is the business willing to pay for a long-term maintenance contract? Either way, companies need to think strategically about the opportunities and implications and ensure that there is internal buy-in from all stakeholders before making the final decision.

When selecting a social or digital agency, a company needs to think strategically and take the time to find the right partner. The importance of long-term business relationships with any agency or business partner should trump any motivation for speed or convenience. Points to consider when seeking such a partnership include these:

- **Scalability**—As the organization grows, the agency can grow as well.

- **Research**—Utilize colleague referrals and Google.

- **Listen**—Spend time understanding the nature of the conversation surrounding the agency. Follow the agency's leadership if it's on Twitter.

- **Act**—Be as specific as possible when developing an RFP. Call the participating agencies to begin establishing some level of rapport.

- **Evaluate**—Make smart decisions and ensure that there is a strong chemistry between the agency and the company.

Probably most important are the agency's core values. Everything an agency does online—everything it says, tweets, and blogs about—is a direct reflection on the clients that the agency represents. This is why it's crucial for organizations to be diligent in hiring the right agency.

8

Marketing Investments on the Rise for Social Business Initiatives

Many times social media teams are forced to roam the halls of corporate America with a tin cup asking for a budget to support social media programs. Either the money has dried up to fund existing programs, a company needs to invest internally in social technologies, or a company needs to hire an agency or community manager to build an external presence in social media.

This scenario usually arises because an organization has not fully evolved into a collaborative social business. A company that has truly embraced social media will do more than just say it does. It will not only transform the culture, break down silos, and build collaborative teams, but it will also add social media programs and funding as a line item to existing marketing budgets.

The good news is that this shift is beginning to happen.

In the last months of 2010, research firms began polling executives and industry leaders to find out what their real plans are for social media programs—they asked about how they'll spend their marketing dollars. The research suggests that the majority of companies are embracing social media, based on their upcoming marketing budgets.

A 2010 report produced by Econsultancy and global digital marketing provider ExactTarget looked in detail at how organizations are allocating their offline and online marketing budgets. Data for the "Marketing Budgets 2010: Effectiveness, Measurement and Allocation Report" was gathered from 1,000 companies in the United States and the United Kingdom between December 2009 and January 2010. The findings show the following:

- 46 percent of companies plan to increase their overall marketing budget for 2010.

- 70 percent of companies plan to increase their budgets for off-site social media programs within networks such as Facebook and Twitter.

Meltwater Group also found that companies are trending toward funding social media efforts. The group's annual report, "2010 Future of Content," focused on research and online monitoring and was conducted in October 2010 through telephone interviews with 450 organizations around the world. Consider Meltwater's findings:

- 40 percent of respondents expect their marketing budgets to go up in 2011, with an average increase of 1.4% forecast.

- In the last 12 months, marketing budgets are most likely to have increased for social media (by 35%), email marketing (by 34%), and online advertising (by 34%).

Additional data from email marketing firm StongMail and Zoomerang reveals an optimistic outlook for marketing investment in social media. They published a report titled "2011 Marketing Trends Survey" that examined the trends and attitudes of 925 business leaders regarding their planned marketing budgets, priorities, and challenges for 2011. Half of the organizations plan to increase marketing budgets, and another 43 percent plan to continue funding at the same level.

Additionally, email and social media marketing remain the top targets for increased spend. The survey found the following:

- 93 percent of respondents plan to increase or maintain their marketing spending in 2011.

- 57 percent of businesses plan to increase their marketing budgets for social media in 2011.

Alterian, a social media monitoring and analysis firm, also recently found that companies intend to allocate more of their marketing budgets to social media programs. In late 2010, Alterian conducted its Eighth Annual Survey, "How Engaged Is Your Brand? 2011," of nearly 1,500 marketers, agencies, marketing services providers (MSPs), and systems integrators (SIs). The survey found these results:

- 57 percent of respondents anticipate an increase in overall marketing spending.

- 75 percent of companies expect that the largest increase in marketing funds will be for social and digital channels.

Social media is top of mind when it comes to not only usage, but also spending, according to research firm eMarketer. A worldwide survey of marketers found that social media ranked third (at 38 percent) among areas marketers planned to target with their online marketing budget in 2011, with search marketing (at 51 percent) and web site optimization (at 47 percent) coming in first and second, respectively.

Finally, the human factor will account for nearly 60 percent of budgets for social media marketing initiatives in 2011, as the MarketingSherpa's "2010 Social Media Marketing Benchmark Report" found. This includes staff salaries for strategy and blogging, content development, and social media monitoring. Another 20 percent of that budget will go outside the organization to hire agencies, consultants, and external social technology vendors.

This multitude of data clearly indicates that marketing investments in social media are becoming top of mind for marketers and business leaders across the United States and abroad in 2011 and moving into 2012. However, companies are still struggling to determine budget needs for social media initiatives. This is mainly because company leadership doesn't understand the value of what social media can do for their organizations. If leaders do understand the value, they're not communicating this throughout the organization through budget planning and forecasting.

While many companies are still trying to figure out social media, some are requiring their marketing and communication teams to demonstrate the business value of using social media before making any financial commitments to support ongoing program and initiatives.

Demonstrating the Business Value of Social Media to Acquire Budget

Business value can mean just about anything. Its meaning depends on the culture of an organization, the industry or vertical, and company leadership.When marketing teams can demonstrate some level of business value from social media, budget increases will surely follow. Along with this rise in budgets, however, will come a rise in expectations from company leadership to produce measurable results.

In fact, almost three out of four CMOs expect to attach revenue assumptions to social media in 2011, even if they hadn't in previous years, according to a 2010 report from Bazaarvoice and the CMO Club. In "CMOs Want Measurable Results from Social Media," 64 percent of CMOs also said they plan to invest more in social media in the next year. This will surely add more pressure to marketing managers to create social media programs that demonstrate a calculated Return on Investment (ROI).

> Along with this rise in budgets, however, will come a rise in expectations from company leadership to produce measurable results.

Despite these expectations, business value doesn't always have to translate into revenue and it shouldn't have to. For many business-to-business (B2B) companies, this is nearly impossible.

Social media results can demonstrate value to the business in a variety of ways; and it's not always measured in terms of dollars earned. Positive publicity and sentiment, collaboration with customers and partners, and increased reach with potential new customers can also demonstrate value to the business.

For example, enterprise application software vendor SAP has embraced and promoted the value of social media and community building for its business. Through the entire business life cycle, from building collaborative software to selling services and solutions to supporting its customers after sales, SAP recognizes a range of results from its social media efforts.

SAP's online community, the SAP Community Network (SCN; see www.sdn.sap.com/irj/scn/index) fulfills many key objectives that ultimately drive business value for SAP. A close examination of the community reveals that it represents a variety of job functions and roles, including developers, engineers, IT and data center professionals, analysts, financial consultants, purchase decision makers, and even end users of SAP products. SAP experts, partners, industry opinion leaders, employees, and customers are collaborating within the community to increase the return on customers' SAP investments.

Mark Yolton, Senior Vice President of the SAP Community Network, wrote in a blog post that "well over 2 million members—with 1.5 million visiting monthly and 100,000 contributing thoughtful solutions and insights—are connecting, collaborating, and sharing for mutual benefit." The SAP Community Network launched more than eight years ago and delivers a wide range of benefits. The community is built on four pillars of business value:

- Social innovation
- Social intelligence
- Social commerce
- Social insight

As Yolton explains in his blog, the SCN is where SAP product managers, engineers, and business leaders can collaborate with customers. They are crowdsourcing new, innovative ideas from the insights of the community. One example is the SAP Idea Place. Similar to Dell's IdeaStorm, the Idea Place helps users to innovate, using a crowdsourcing tool hosted by SAP that enables customers and partners give input on SAP products at all phases of development, from design to testing to updates. SAP product managers get direct, real-time, customer-driven feedback on specific projects; input on requested features and functionality in current products; and, in some cases, ideas for entirely new products.

Business intelligence in general is key to making data-driven decisions. Intelligence acquired from the community will not only drive decision making, but also shape future products offerings. IT and research and development (R&D) organizations are using this actionable intelligence to equip their teams to develop precise business cases for technology solutions, provide the best approaches to solve technical challenges, and create best practices in business operations.

This is true of the SAP community. Today the SCN has 6,000 active bloggers, most of which are not even SAP employees, but customers and partners. These bloggers are sharing their concerns, best practices, technology challenges, and implementation ideas with the broader community. This real-time intelligence is valuable for SAP in innovating and improving its product offerings which demonstrates serious business value for EMC executives.

Time is money. In today's real-time business environment, organizations need to evaluate technology solutions and make timely decisions. Community members who participate in the SCN are learning about each other's implementations of SAP technologies and partner products. The time needed to evaluate technology solutions then dramatically decreases. As with most professional communities, a high degree of trust exists between its members. When sourcing for a technology solution provider, customers have a reliable source—other SAP customers—to help them assess their technology challenges and even make purchase decisions. This level of trust is imperative when sourcing technology solutions. The SAP EcoHub provides SAP customers with this option.

Within the EcoHub, customers can discover new technology solutions, get real-time feedback from their peers within the community, access online demos and customer reviews, and even initiate the purchase of SAP solutions directly within that area of the community.

Intelligence becomes insight when used to evolve business operations and change behavior. Within the SCN, SAP is actively observing and engaging with community members. The company is listening to community discussions and feedback and extracting intelligence from these discussions. By using this intelligence, SAP can better change a product or service, as well as equip sales teams with actionable information that can help them best meet the needs of customers and even markets. Additionally, the right quantitative and qualitative analysis offers deep insight into customer pain points, technology challenges, and new opportunities that equip engineers with information on which features and functionality customers will demand and buy in the future. This analysis also turns up customer support issues that evolve from community discussions.

Evidence that the SAP Community Network demonstrates business value becomes visible when customers are vocal about their personal experiences. Phillip Parkinson, integration developer at Standard Bank, says this about SCN:

> [W]ith the SAP Community Network, we're able to capitalize on the content and lessons learned to significantly shorten our learning curve and development life cycles.

This SAP example can be used as a guide for companies that are trying to determine the business value that social media can bring to their organizations. With minimal investment, enterprise companies can create external communities for customers and partners to engage and share key learning and technology challenges with each other.

For the community to successfully show business value, however, company leaders must be committed to empowering their employees to engage in community discussions. More importantly, companies need to be committed to apply the collective intelligence gathered from these discussions to their products offerings and business operations.

SAP is doing just that. Its community engagement efforts are helping drive innovation, intelligence gathering, sales leads, and insights into business operations and sales development life cycles. It's safe to assume that, over the last eight years, budget investments have increased and are now part of ongoing financial discussions internally.

Given recent research and SAP's experience with the SCN, it comes as no surprise that marketing budgets are beginning to increase for social media investments. However, it's important to understand how businesses are prioritizing their budgets and exactly which job functions these investments are being allocated to.

How Organizations Are Prioritizing Social Media Budgets

After budgets are acquired for social media, many companies and business leaders aren't quite sure where to make the investment. Some are focusing on investments in internal technologies—for example, community applications and CRM. Others are using those dollars to hire agencies and putting more focus on external engagement efforts.

In 2010, Jeremiah Owyang and Charlene Li, partners at Altimeter Group, released a report titled "How Corporations Should Prioritize Social Business Budgets." The data was gathered from more than 140 global social media marketers in September and October 2010. One of the key findings was that corporate spending on social media initiatives averaged $833,000 in 2010. A closer examination of the data reveals the following:

- Companies with revenue earnings less than $250 million spent $229,000 on social media.

- Companies with revenue earnings between $250 million and $1 billion spent $408,000 on social media.

- Companies with revenue earnings between $1 billion and $10 billion spent $568,000 on social media.

- Companies with revenue earnings of more than $10 billion spent about $2 million on social media.

It may seem natural to assume that the more an organization earns in revenue, the more it would naturally spend on marketing-related activities. This is not the case, though. Social media investments specifically correlate to program maturity levels, according to Altimeter.

In the survey, social strategists were asked to classify their social media programs by maturity level: novice, intermediate, and advanced. The data found that 52 percent were classified as intermediate, 23 percent were advanced, and 25 percent were novice.

One of the key findings in the report is that overall social media budgets increase as the organization matures and evolves into a social business. This makes perfect sense when examining this insight holistically. To be effective, the social business evolution has to become an integral part of an organization's DNA—its culture. This means that employees at every level must incorporate social behaviors into how they work every day, regardless of their job function. The end result is technology investments in internal communities and collaboration platforms, as well as investment in staff hired to deploy the applications, community managers and strategists, and staff that externally engages with the social customer.

Altimeter's data also revealed that adoption of social media initiatives, coupled with spending, will certainly increase in the coming years. Much of the investment falls into three categories: internal soft costs, customer-facing initiatives, and technology investments.

Internal soft costs include hiring community managers, strategists, analysts, and managers who will mainly be responsible for deploying and overseeing social media initiatives. This also includes costs related to training, organizational development, and research and development. Customer-facing initiatives include marketing dollars allocated to paid media programs within social media channels, investments in influencer programs, and contracts with external digital or PR agencies. Technology investments include both internal and external applications used to deploy and manage social media programs. (Chapter 2, "Surveying the Technology Supermarket," discusses several of these technology vendors and categorizes them by internal communities/collaboration, social CRM, social listening, and social relationship management applications.)

Altimeter concludes the report with seven social business adoption initiatives that companies should consider when making financial investments:

- Organizations will ramp up hiring efforts to manage social media initiatives, but investment in training and organizational development will be low.

- Marketing teams will invest heavily in paid media within social media networks.

- Companies that fall into the advanced category will spend more on hiring agencies to help with strategy, deployment, and execution of social media programs.

- Most organizations will make technology investments in social listening software.

- Companies will continue to invest in community platforms and leverage the networks for customer support and marketing efforts.

- Companies that fall into the advanced category will integrate social media platforms into the corporate website.

- To scale, mature programs will invest in social media relationship-management systems and social CRM applications.

The key takeaways from this study by Altimeter are that every company is different and manages its budgets differently, depending on the size of the organization, its culture, its maturity level, and its company leadership. However, the trends listed previously are good indicators that companies are slowly moving through the social business adoption life-cycle and will naturally invest more dollars into social business initiatives.

What's important to remember is that change needs to start internally to have the most impact externally. This means that organizations that are in the novice or advanced stages in the social business adoption life cycle should focus their investments on getting their internal houses in order first. This means that budget focus should be not only on hiring people to manage social media, but also on training existing employees in how to engage with the social customers, ways to use

collaboration and communications applications, social etiquette, and
so on. Internal community deployment should also be a key focus
when it comes time for budget planning. This certainly doesn't imply
that companies should abandon all external social media programs—
just that the focus should be on the foundation of a social business, the
organization.

How to Determine Budgets for Social Media

Organizations allocate budgets based on their maturity level and size.
What's not explained in the Altimeter study is *why* companies are not
maturing in the social business adoption life cycle. Much of the "why"
relates to a lack of confidence and experience; a company might not
be ready for change and might not be willing to make significant
investments into social business initiatives. The companies that are
spending millions of dollars in paid media advertising are allocating
very small percentages to social media and even smaller budgets
to change management, which is a key pillar to social business
transformation.

In many organizations, social media budgets are being formed out of
funds already allocated to the overall marketing budget, which
includes paid media, web site development, public relations, and so on.
Social media marketers often have to fight tooth and nail to justify
budget increases every quarter. In other cases, a bucket of money
somewhere in the accounting books might be set aside for social
media pilot programs. Both of these scenarios are ineffective and will
not scale as a company matures.

This is why marketers and business leaders must think about the long-
term opportunities social media can bring to the organization, as well
as the opportunity costs of ignoring it. When faced with budget decisions, marketers must consider several questions:

- What are the company's business and marketing goals? Will
  social media programs (internal and external) contribute to
  the goals? If not, maybe social media engagement is not the
  right channel.

- Will a budget be set aside for research? Without data or some
  level of insight, companies are taking a shot in the dark.

- What are the organization's internal strengths and weak-nesses? Are employees, customer support teams, or commu-nity managers ready and able to engage? If not, will some of the budget be set aside for hiring and training?

- What resources are available to support social media initia-tives? Who will write content and moderate comments? What is the editorial plan for Facebook and Twitter? Are technical applications available to support it?

- Is there a need to hire an agency? Better yet, does the existing agency have the skill set and thought leadership to support social media initiatives? These are considerations that are important when thinking about budgets.

After answering these questions, marketers and business leaders will be better equipped to make budget decisions for social media and help determine where the funds will actually come from. In many cases, the social media budgets could be taken out of an organization other than marketing.

For example, funds might come from an IT budget to deploy a social media application with a tool such as Jive. This makes sense because a team of IT engineers and developers will likely be responsible for the deployment, management, and ongoing maintenance of the commu-nity application. The budget allocated to this may certainly be a shared expense with other organizations, depending on the company.

Externally, customer support organizations might have the budget responsibility of external support communities, community engage-ment, investments in social listening software, and reporting. This naturally makes sense because much of the customer support organi-zation would be using these communities and tools to address and engage with the social customer.

In many organizations, community managers and the budgets associ-ated with their job responsibilities will come from a product organiza-tion. It's a best practice for community managers to have extensive knowledge about the company's products and services. Many commu-nity managers today also were previously product managers. Not only does this product knowledge help them engage more effectively with the community and share content, but it also gives them knowledge for answering technical support questions.

In a perfect world, companies will think about budgets that can help them socialize their business operations first. But the reality is that most companies are working backward. That is, they already have budgets they are using to engage in Facebook and Twitter. They already have corporate blogs and community managers, and many of them are using paid media to drive traffic and engagement to their branded communities. These companies are displaying characteristics of a social brand. The issue today is that these same companies are realizing the internal challenges of collaboration, culture change, employee communications, executive support, and so on. They are tasked with determining budgets to address this and help them evolve to a social business.

Taking the Next Steps

As companies' use of social media continues to explode around the world, the social media landscape will continue to see massive change. Companies are determining their strategic initiatives, which include budget investments.

Business leaders, marketers, and other decision makers need to recognize this shift early and begin planning for budget allocations in social media spending. Understanding the trends is just as important. An eMarketer study in 2010 revealed the industries that forecast the biggest budget increases in the United States. Almost 80 percent of retail and e-commerce firms will increase their social media budgets. In addition, 69 percent of publishing/media companies, 55 percent of technology hardware and software vendors, 54 percent of business and consumer services providers, 54 percent of manufacturing and packaged goods companies, 52 percent of travel companies, and 43 percent of education and healthcare organizations also expect to increase their budgets for social media. Knowledge and understanding of these trends is key to staying ahead of the competition. More important, though, is for companies to take action—and this means spending budget dollars wisely and making a commitment to adding social business initiatives to ongoing marketing budgets.

Additionally, organizations need to allocate much of their budget dollars internally to operationalize different areas of business, such as hiring, social technology investments, and customer support. A 2010 eMarketer report stated that 60 percent of social media marketing dollars next year will go toward staff salaries for activities such as blogging, developing content, and monitoring social channels. Another two-fifths will be spent on outside help from agencies, consultancies, and service providers. This area of investment is critical to the success of a social business.

When thinking about budgets, think Facebook. According to MarketingSherpa's "2010 Social Media Marketing Benchmark Report," social media budgets will be spent with the social network of choice: Facebook. The report examines other social networks, such as MySpace, which received $490 million in advertising spending but is predicted to decrease by 21 percent over the next year. Facebook, on the other hand, will increase by 39 percent and is being forced to expand its service offerings to give companies new opportunities to engage fans and build community. In December 2010, Mark Zuckerberg, founder of Facebook, told the world on *60 Minutes* that anything a person can do online, he can do on Facebook: shopping, searching, poking, stalking, chatting, blogging, emailing, collaborating, and more. Marketers need to keep this in mind when planning for long-term social media initiatives. They should focus on Facebook as a marketing channel.

> Organizations need to allocate much of their budget dollars internally to operationalize different areas of business, such as hiring, social technology investments, and customer support.

As marketers begin to think about allocating budgets, Facebook should certainly be a consideration. It's no surprise that Facebook's revenue for advertising added up to an astonishing $1.86 billion for 2010. In fact, in an interview with AdAge, eMarketer analyst Debra Williamson said that around 60 percent of Facebook's 2010 ad revenue came from small to medium-size business (SMBs). In addition, $740 million of Facebook's revenue in 2010 came from major brands, such as Procter & Gamble and Coca-Cola. Williamson also said that Facebook alone accounted for 5 percent of all online advertising spending in 2010, and she predicted that this number will rise to 8 percent in 2011.

Finally, as social media budgets increase, so will the expectations from senior management to provide some level of business value or measurable return on investment (ROI). Chapter 6, "Establishing a Measurement Philosophy," gives insight into how organizations can calculate financial impact metrics such as ways to measure paid, earned, and owned media values; strict ROI metrics; and even cost savings in using social media for customer support.

Additionally, other ways to think about demonstrating business value can include positive publicity and sentiment, collaboration with customers and partners, innovation of business processes, products and service offerings based on community feedback, and increased reach with potential new customers.

9

Creating a Comprehensive Social Media Strategic Plan

Contrary to popular belief, crafting a social media strategy is actually the last step in the process of becoming a social business. First, a company must become completely aligned internally; that is, it has completely evolved into a more collaborative and integrated structure. It has comprehensively defined ownership of the social media function, established a governance model, and sourced and selected technology partners and agencies.

Creating a social media strategic plan is a comprehensive and detailed task that organizations handle in a variety of ways, depending on their size and structure. Some companies create a strategy that encompasses an entire fiscal year and then create smaller (or more tactical) quarterly execution plans that align with the strategy. The strategy is sometimes referred to as a "plan of record." In some cases, the plan is a living document and goes through a natural evolution process as the external social landscape changes or the organization itself experiences management changes.

Other companies are less formal and create a "mission" or "charter" for the social media function and then plan for quarterly strategies or tactical plans. The benefit of this approach is that it allows the plan to be more flexible and to change direction quickly. Often companies with this mindset are more open to trying new and unproven approaches in the social space. Of course, the downfall is that not all plans may be aligned with consistent messaging, which can result in customer confusion and subpar social media programs. Both approaches can work just as effectively. It just depends on the organization's culture and planning cycles.

Companies must consider several points when creating a social media strategic plan for it to deliver business value and be as comprehensive as possible. Critical components include a clearly defined mission, defined goals and objectives, and a tactical approach. Understanding the target audience members and the way they interact in social media environments across various global regions is equally important. In addition, the plan must include integration points with paid media (or advertising), along with a clear definition of the key performance indicators (KPIs).

> Companies must consider several points when creating a social media strategic plan for it to deliver business value and be as comprehensive as possible.

Defining the Mission, Goals, Objectives, Strategy, and Tactics for a Social Media Plan

To be a truly effective social business, the entire organization must speak the same language. Confusion sometimes arises when defining business language, especially with social media. Companies need to clearly understand the definitions of mission, goals, strategy, and tactics to avoid confusion with the planning process.

The Mission of Social Media

The mission statement is the focal point of the strategic plan, so it must be clear. A mission, sometimes referred to as a "team charter," is a short statement of the company's purpose or vision, or a high-level result or achievement. Mission statements identify the nonfinancial achievement that a CEO, group head, or manager wants the company, product, or team to pursue. The mission addresses the "what" versus the "how" and is used to determine the organization's direction and guide decision-making. The following examples are mission statements from two Fortune 500 companies, Cisco and Dell:

> Shape the future of the Internet by creating unprecedented value and opportunity for our customers, employees, investors, and ecosystem partners.

> Dell's mission is to be the most successful computer company in the world at delivering the best customer experience in markets we serve.

Most teams in charge of social media have their own mission and use it to steer all their marketing plans. This mission can include statements such as the following:

- Create business value using community engagement that will increase conversational volume, share of voice, sentiment, and engagement in owned and earned media properties.

- Forge meaningful, collaborative relationship with influencers, advocates, and the target audience.

- Become a content machine by creating, co-creating, distributing, and amplifying relevant branded content.

- Activate targeted advertising, promotions, and sponsorships, and driving contextually relevant social conversations that extend the value and opportunity of paid digital advertising.

The mission will depend on the roles and responsibilities of the social media team as well as the size and culture of the company. For example, a business-to-business (B2B) company will have a very different mission than a business-to-consumer (B2C) company. Nonetheless, documenting a mission and ensuring that the entire team, business unit, and company support that mission is critical.

The Social Goals and Objectives

Goals and objectives are synonymous and are used interchangeably in the business environment. These are the stated, measurable targets (or outcomes) in achieving a particular task and are closely aligned with the mission. Goals and objectives also address the "what" versus the "how" but are more specific and actionable than a mission. The most commonly used framework for establishing goals is the SMART framework, first used by George T. Doran in 1981:

- **Specific**—Goals must be simple and specific, as in "to increase awareness and consideration about the brand."

- **Measurable**—Goals must be measurable so that the company can determine whether the goal was met. An example of a measurable goal is "to increase awareness and consideration about the brand by 10 percent." Simply adding a quantitative value to a goal ensures that it can be measured.

- **Achievable**—This aspect might require a look back at historical data, such as growth rates or previous sales revenue. Certainly, creating an unreachable goal isn't wise, but goals also must be set high enough to ensure adequate business value and return on investment.

- **Relevant**—Goals must be challenging but also tightly integrated with the company and team mission.

- **Time-specific**—Goals must have a limit for achievement, such as "by the end of the fiscal year."

If a social media team's mission is to create business value through engagement by driving conversational volume, share of voice, sentiment, and engagement on the social web, a practical example of a goal using the SMART framework might look something like this:

> We want to increase awareness, consideration, and conversation on the social web about the brand by 65 percent in the next quarter.

The Social Strategy

A strategy is an idea. It takes into consideration the organizational (or team) goals and devises a plan. It addresses the "how" versus the "what." A strategy is a conceptualization and plan of action for how to achieve a goal or objective at a very high level. Many companies today hire strategists to devise marketing plans. They are essentially the "thinkers" who can look at the big picture when trying to solve real business problems. Some companies today hire social media strategists for this responsibility and then rely on an agency, junior staff, or community managers (or doers) to execute the plan. In some organizations, the entire social media plan and execution is outsourced to an agency.

Building upon the previous mission statement and goal of increasing awareness and consideration about the brand, this could be an associated strategy:

> Empower employees to engage online with influencers and the general community.

Social Media Tactical Plans

Tactics are the specific actions taken to achieve the goals, in close alignment with the strategy. In most cases, a tactic addresses the "what" and "how," depending on how the goals are framed. In some cases, tactics are included in the "execution plan." Tactics are primarily executed by "doers," in the form of junior staff, agencies, or community managers. Although execution is more about doing than thinking, it's still a critical part of any plan because poor execution prevents a company from achieving its business goals. In the earlier example of empowering employees to engage online with influencers, viable tactics to support the strategy would include these:

- Create social media policies that address employees' behavior when engaging online.

- Train employees on how to blog, use Twitter, and be conversational when interacting in the community.

- Develop a metrics model to measure the effectiveness of employee engagement on the social web.

- Find and engage with online influencers and the communities where they spend their time, using social listening software.

Closely examining the tactics will reveal that they are all actionable and aligned with the mission, goals, and strategy.

Understanding Audience Segmentation

When devising a social media strategic plan, it's imperative to include who the target audience members are and how they use social media. For example, a company that sells hair products for 25- to 34-year-old women might need to categorize them into different subgroups, such as single women, married women with or without children, mommy bloggers, and working women. This can help prioritize the importance of each group and create tactical programs that speak to each segment in a relevant voice.

Some organizations go through an exhaustive audience segmentation process to ensure that they are as relevant as possible when going to market with their social plans. Audience segmentation is a process of categorizing the overall target audience into smaller segments or subgroups. Many times these subgroups have fictitious names for internal reference.

For example, Post Cereals, which manufactures popular cereals such as Cocoa Puffs and Raisin Bran, might have a target audience of general consumers. A segmentation analysis, however, might reveal more specific traits to classify each consumer into groups:

- General demographics, such as age, ethnicity, and income

- Buying habits and behaviors

- What they read and how they interact with friends and neighbors

- Where they shop (for example, online or at the grocery store) and who is responsible for making purchase decisions

Traditionally, moms have been the primary decision makers in homes when it comes to making purchasing decisions for groceries. Moms also are often the ones who do the actual shopping. So it's probably safe to assume that one segment of Post's target audience consists of moms, right?

Actually, in a 2010 study by Yahoo!, interviews of 2,400 U.S. 18- to 64-year-old men identified that demographic as the primary grocery shoppers in their homes. For Post, this might well be an additional audience segment. Insights similar to this are valuable and probably can only be revealed by a segmentation study, which, like the preceding example, will shed some light on which segment a company should be targeting.

For a B2B company such as Silicon Valley networking company Cisco, a segmentation analysis can uncover similar information. Obvious Cisco target customers are business professionals or people working in an enterprise. But "business professionals" in the enterprise can be categorized in many ways, and a segmentation analysis can reveal more specific details about them. These customers can be grouped based on answers to these questions:

- What is their job title, and what are they responsible for? Are they a network engineer, data center architect, or chief information officer (CIO)? Are they responsible for making purchase decisions? Do they manage a team?

- What type or publications do they read? Where do they spend their time online?

- How many years of experience do they have? What is their natural job growth pattern?

- What are their daily work-related activities?

An audience segmentation analysis is important because it allows marketers to accurately plan for segment priorities, messaging, and social media usage and behaviors. The end result of a segmentation study is relevancy—that is, the more specific details a company knows about its target audience, the more relevant it can be with messaging and programs.

One useful segmentation analysis is Forrester's Social Technographic Profile Ladder of Participation. It categorizes consumers' use of social technologies and their general behavior online. According to this method of analysis, consumers are segmented into seven different groups:

> An audience segmentation analysis is important because it allows marketers to accurately plan for segment priorities, messaging, and social media usage and behaviors.

- **Creators**—Create and publish content on blogs, Twitter, and YouTube.

- **Critics**—Post ratings and reviews on websites such as ePinions, Yelp, and CNET. These users also comment on various blogs and wikis and contribute to online forums.

- **Collectors**—Collect content in the form of tags and RSS feeds. They also vote for content on websites such as Digg.com.

- **Joiners**—Join social networks but might not necessarily create or interact with any content.

- **Spectators**—Only consume content. They read blogs, watch videos, read customer reviews, and listen to podcasts.

- **Inactives**—Don't create or consume any social content whatsoever.

Using Forrester's free social technographics tool (which can be found at www.forrester.com/empowered/tool_consumer.html), and considering the earlier example of a company that sells hair products targeting U.S. women ages 25 to 34, the results tell a specific story about this segment: Thirty-one percent of all women in the United States are creators, 43 percent are critics, 24 percent are collectors, 74 percent are joiners, and 78 percent are spectators.

Although this data is very high level and general, companies can use it to make specific decisions when creating social media programs. Because 74 percent of this segment actively "joins" social networks, it wouldn't be a bad idea for a company to explore building a community for this segment or simply launching a Facebook fan page. Additionally, building in functionality that enables users to rate content or review products might be an option because 43 percent are critics and are familiar with this type of online behavior.

A company can add value to a Technographics Profile by mapping specific behaviors to specific segments. And this is where the social media agency or consulting firm can come in and support the plan. One aspect to consider when facilitating an audience segmentation study is the global landscape. This is important for global businesses that are considering using social media specifically for their individual regions.

Global Considerations of Social Media

Social media has to be locally driven. This simply means that what works in the United States, for example, will not necessarily work in other parts of the world. One quick illustration is Twitter. Although Twitter is used widely in the U.S. and growing in popularity, parts of Asia do not use Twitter at all. Before companies can think about launching social media programs, they must spend time understanding the local market trends, as well as the way consumers are using social technologies in each of the countries and regions where they are considering.

Research firms such as ComScore, Nielsen, Altimeter, and Forrester already provide comprehensive case studies and research that outline usage models, social media adoption, and platform analysis globally.

Many of these studies are free to download and use, but the more comprehensive and in-depth studies come with a fee. The only exception is data from Altimeter Group, which publishes all its research free of charge for public consumption.

GlobalWebIndex provides a self-service online tool that helps companies, agencies, and business professionals understand their target audience, business category, and market trends in each region of the world. The tool pulls data from a sample size of 51,000 Internet users from 18 different countries. In 2011, the sample size will increase to 90,000 Internet users and cover 20 key online markets. The data set focuses on consumer web behavior and adoption across browser-based technologies and packaged web platforms, social media adoption and impact, attitudes and motivations regarding the role of the Internet, perception and needs for brands online, and the models for content delivery and monetization.

A 2011 breakdown of social media activity in Europe, Latin America, and Asia-Pacific using data from GlobalWebIndex, ComScore, and Nielsen reveals some interesting trends in social network growth, adoption, and user behavior.

Snapshot of Social Media Usage in Europe

In Europe, 60 percent of all social network users had an active profile on Facebook at the end of 2010, which equals a little more than 69 million people. Facebook is the most dominant social media network across Europe, but several country-specific social networks are popular as well. One of these is Odnoklassniki, in Russia; 10 percent of European social network users have an active profile on Odnoklassniki, even thought it's dedicated to Russian-speaking users.

It's no surprise that Facebook has become the top social network in most European countries. Part of this growth resulted from Facebook introducing a translated version of the site in January 2008.

A closer examination of the activities of social network users in Europe shows the extent to which messaging services on social networks are replacing traditional email services. Seventy percent of European social network users have sent messages to friends via a social network, 64 percent have uploaded photos to their social network, and 52 percent have watched an online video via a social network service. Yet while 42 percent of users have joined a group on a social network, just 16 percent of those social media users have joined a group that is affiliated with a brand or product. This might seem discouraging for companies operating in Europe, but it's also a huge opportunity to begin thinking about expanding in the European market.

A more in-depth analysis using GlobalWebIndex showed that European users spend a lot of time within their social networks and engage in a variety of different behaviors:

- 27% installed applications within their social network.
- 41% played a game within their social network.
- 20% sent a digital or virtual gift to a friend.
- 23% uploaded a video to their social network profile.
- 52% watched a video shared by a friend.
- 18% wrote a blog.

Outside their social networks, European users are also engaged in social media:

- 31% left a comment on a website or blog.
- 27% posted a comment within a forum or message board.
- 20% uploaded a video online.
- 39% uploaded a photo online.
- 9% used a microblogging service, such as Twitter.
- 63% watched a video.
- 13% actively wrote a blog.

Additionally, In 2010, ComScore reported that Twitter growth in Europe soared 106 percent from the previous year's figures, to 22.5 million total visitors accessing Twitter.com.

Snapshot of Social Media Usage in Latin America

In Latin America, Facebook has a strong market position compared to other networks. Fifty-five percent of Latin American social network users have an active Facebook profile. Surprisingly, 83 percent of Latin American social network users also have an active profile on Orkut (mostly in Brazil), which is a social network owned by Google, and another 40 percent have an active profile on Windows Live Spaces; both of those audiences are much higher than in other regions around the world. The *Latin Business Chronicle* reports that there were ninety-five million Facebook users in Latin America as of March 2011.

Despite the difference in platform usage, the activities of Latin American social media users are similar to those of European and Asia-Pacific (APAC) users. Seventy-three percent of Latin American social network users send messages via their favorite social networks. Sixty-six percent of users are active on instant-messaging services via social networks, and 62 percent have uploaded and shared photos on a social network. Similar to European users, a low 21 percent of social network users have joined a social network group affiliated with a brand or product, and only 5 percent have joined a branded community.

Data from GlobalWebIndex suggests that Latin American users spend a lot of time within their social networks and engage in a variety of different behaviors:

- 47% installed applications within their social network.

- 47% played a game within their social network.

- 30% sent a digital or virtual gift to a friend.

- 38% uploaded a video to their social network profile.

- 68% watched a video shared by a friend.

- 26% wrote a blog.

Outside their social networks, Latin America users are also engaged in social media usage:

- 49% left a comment on a website or blog.

- 35% posted a comment within a forum or message board.

- 41% uploaded a video online.

- 56% uploaded a photo online.

- 25% used a microblogging service such as Twitter.

- 74% watched a video.

- 27% actively wrote a blog.

Finally, a study by ComScore calculated that 15 million Internet users in Latin America visited Twitter.com from work or home computers in June 2010, representing growth of 305 percent over the previous year. What's more, this number excludes the millions of users who accessed Twitter through third-party mobile and desktop client applications such as TweetDeck, HootSuite, and Seesmic.

Snapshot of Social Media Usage in Asia-Pacific Countries (APAC)

In Asia-Pacific countries, social media usage is increasing and reaching a wider audience than ever. However, Facebook doesn't dominate social media as much as in other regions. Because of government bans in countries such as China, only 32 percent of APAC social network users have an active profile on Facebook. This is still a sizeable user base, however, equating to nearly 71 million users.

In China, the largest APAC market covered in the GlobalWebIndex, QZone (a social network created by Tencent in 2005) and RenRen (a social network with very similar features to Facebook) are the most popular social networks, and 36 percent and 24 percent of Chinese social network users have an active profile within these social networks, respectively.

Activities that APAC users undertake on their social networks are much the same as in Europe. For example, 64 percent of APAC social network users send messages via the social network platform. Furthermore, 66 percent upload and share photos, and 52 percent watch videos on their social network platforms. One interesting difference is found in the proportion of social network users writing blogs; 53 percent of APAC users write a blog on a social network, compared to just 18 percent of European users.

APAC users also spend a lot of time within their social networks and are just as engaged as users in Europe and Latin America:

- 43% installed applications within their social network.
- 55% played a game within their social network.
- 30% sent a digital or virtual gift to a friend.
- 35% uploaded a video to their social network profile.
- 52% watched a video shared by a friend.
- 53% wrote a blog.

Outside their social networks, APAC users are also engaged in social media usage:

- 42% left a comment on a website or blog.
- 43% posted a comment within a forum or message board.
- 29% uploaded a video online.
- 50% uploaded a photo online.
- 26% use a microblogging service such as Twitter.
- 65% watched a video.
- 37% actively wrote a blog.

A 2010 study by ComScore reported that Facebook is the leader for many of the individual markets in Asia-Pacific. India, Japan, South Korea, and Taiwan have their own local social networking sites that dominate market share. A similar ComScore study revealed that Twitter grew 243 percent, to 25.1 million visitors. Numbers for the Middle East and Africa jumped 142 percent, to 5 million visitors.

In 2010, Nielsen released a similar study titled "Social Media Dominates Asia Pacific Internet Usage" and reported unprecedented growth among Asia-Pacific countries. The report found that three of the seven largest global online brands are social media sites, including Facebook, Wikipedia, and YouTube. Additionally, the influence of social media has a significant impact on consumers' purchasing behavior. In Asia-Pacific countries, online product reviews are the third-most-trusted source of information when making purchase decisions, behind family and friends. The report also uncovered several insights for companies to consider before going to market in these regions.

Blogging is exploding in Japan. Japanese Internet users are the most prolific bloggers globally, posting more than a million blog posts per month. Their adoption of Twitter continues to grow as well, with unique visitor numbers increasing from less than 200,000 in 2009 to more than 10 million in 2010.

Although 70 percent of social media users in India identify Orkut as their preferred social network, Facebook is gaining market share, with 50 percent of social media users claiming to use Facebook most often, compared to 38 percent for Orkut. Additionally, Twitter has experienced explosive growth in India: Fifty-seven percent of Twitter users signed up in the past year. In addition, 32 percent of India's social media users use Twitter at least once a day.

Social media use is on the rise in South Korea. Naver, the leading social network site, attracts nearly 95 percent of the Korean Internet population every month. Twitter experienced 1,900 percent growth during the reporting period.

Although regional data is good to know from a high level perspective, it's not nearly as granular when examining country-specific data and trends. Even though countries are a part of the same region, the usage models and social media behaviors differ dramatically when comparing one country to another. For this reason, it is crucial for companies that are expanding globally to understand the target audience in each country where they plan to launch operations. Understanding which networks are widely used in each country and region helps organizations plan accordingly for global expansion.

Integrating Social Media with Owned and Paid Media

From a paid media perspective, the opportunities are endless for social media integration. One of the benefits of paid media is that it can potentially reach millions of people quickly. Any company can easily create a Google AdWords account, add a budget, and begin to sell products and capture some real estate on the search engine results page. It's just as easy to get on the phone with a sales rep at Mashable, TechCrunch, or Federated Media to discuss a paid media program.

The value that social media brings to paid media is relevancy. Most traditional display advertising campaigns require rounds of approvals from the brand marketing teams and the legal department to ensure that the marketing message stays "on brand" and doesn't make any unsubstantiated claims. This process holds true for most corporate websites as well. However, if done right, paid media can help jump-start a branded community, increase a company's Twitter following, and grow Facebook "Likes."

As mentioned in Chapter 1, "Human Capital, Evolved," individuals trust people like themselves. They distrust advertising and corporate communications. A truly integrated social and paid media program encompasses some elements of a relevant conversation in the form of blog posts, tweets, discussions on a Facebook page, or some other type of user-generated content.

For example, when Intel released its Centrino 2 processor in 2008, it used several marketing channels to increase awareness about the launch, with paid media leading the way. One tactic that proved successful was creating a 300×250 display ad unit that integrated a real-time RSS feed from an Intel blog. Each blog post in the unit was specific to Centrino 2 and written by Intel social media practitioners. On average, click-through rates (CTR) for display ads range from just 0.2 to 0.3 percent; this equates to only two to three clicks out of every 1,000 impressions (or people who see the unit). In this case, the CTR was a little over 5 percent. The ad unit had to be pulled down almost immediately because it caused mass server load issues and the server eventually went down.

Ford Motor Company also exemplifies marrying paid media with social media marketing. In 2011, Ford released a print advertisement in *Architectural Digest* magazine highlighting a screenshot of a specific discussion on Ford's Facebook fan page. One of Ford's fans had asked about the difference between the performance of the 2011 2.5 V6 and the 2010 4.6 V8. The entire messaging on the print ad addressed his question and suggested that the new 2011 Ford was powerful and efficient.

Integrating social media with owned and paid media channels isn't hard to do. In fact, it can be executed relatively easily, as long as there's cooperation among marketing teams. One way to do this is to make the corporate website more social. Simply adding the Facebook "Like" widget on the home page or product pages is an easy way to make the corporate website more relevant. Many companies today are adding hyperlinks to Facebook at the bottom of the home page. This is definitely a start; however, few Internet users scroll down a web page and read marketing copy on a corporate website. Ensuring that the social integration happens "above the fold" is ideal. The "Like" widget might not necessarily match the brand's look and feel, but users relate more to each other than they do marketing copy, and the widget provides a level of humanity needed for social relevancy.

Companies can take it one step further and integrate a Twitter feed directly into their website by using specified hashtags or pulling in tweets from the corporate and employees' Twitter accounts. Another option is to pull in relevant blog posts to product pages.

Featuring brand advocates on the corporate website is another way to achieve social integration. By showcasing premoderated, user-generated content, companies can let their advocates tell the brand story using their own, authentic voices.

In addition, many companies are sponsoring third-party websites such as College Humor, the Oprah Winfrey Network, and CNET, to maximize their presence within these networks. They're buying media placements throughout the website and sending users to a branded "hub" or microsite. To maximize the traffic to these hubs, companies need to pull in their existing owned media channels, such as Facebook, Twitter, or corporate blogs and communities. This helps grow the community with users who are already interested in the brand, product, or service.

Taking the Next Steps

Creating a social media strategic plan isn't easy to do. It requires strong partnerships internally, collaboration among various marketing teams, research, and smart thinking. The ability to think beyond just "social" is necessary because social media alone will not yield the business results that companies require in this competitive market.

Having a clear and documented mission of the role of social media is key in setting the foundation for the entire strategy. A quick military analogy further illustrates the difference in a mission, goals and objectives, strategy, and tactics:

- **Mission**—World domination.

- **Goal**—Win the war against our opponent in the next 12 months.

- **Strategy**—Decrease the morale of enemy troops.

- **Tactics**—Wipe out all the enemy communication lines. Destroy all fuel and supply routes. Take out enemy leadership.

More important than defining and documenting each of these elements within a PowerPoint slide deck is the ability to articulately and confidently explain how these components work together. Explain, too, how social media drives overall business value.

When companies consider expanding globally, the natural conclusion is that the core focus should be on Facebook and Twitter. This might be the case, but it makes wise business sense to first understand and study the specific country market data and social media usage models before spending significant time, budget, and resources trying to build a social media program there.

Equally important is studying how consumers behave with the social technologies that they use every day. If a natural behavior is reading blog content and watching video, it makes sense for a program to potentially include a blog featuring video.

First understand and study the specific country market data and social media usage models before spending significant time, budget, and resources trying to build a social media program there.

Additionally, organizations need to realize that social content cannot be translated and used across various geographies. This is especially important when developing global social media plans. Many companies today are approaching this in two ways.

Some firms are simply publishing content in English. However, although English is considered the global language of business, it might not be a preferred method for consuming content on the social web. In addition, users might naturally search for content in Google (or other search engines) in their native language. If a company is posting content only in English, it will miss the opportunity to be found in the search results. The end result will be no web traffic, no engagement, and complete irrelevance.

Other companies are translating existing blog content, Facebook status updates, and tweets to the local language. On the surface, this might seem like a viable practice, and most corporate websites follow this same practice. The challenge is that social media content is usually informal, full of jargon, and centered on personal and cultural anecdotes. Direct, word-for-word translation doesn't work.

Before expanding into a different geography, companies also must have local on-the-ground support in that specific geography, to maximize the effectiveness of any social media strategy. Simply put, if a company doesn't have adequate support in the form of strategists, community managers, or employees willing to engage with customers online and in that region, launching a social media initiative might not be the right way to proceed.

Finally social media cannot operate in a silo. To maximize the effectiveness of any social media strategy, a company needs some level of paid and owned media integration. From a business perspective, it makes sense to leverage all the internal assets at a company's disposal. From a marketing perspective, having an integrated plan with consistent messaging globally is the icing on the cake.

10

The Rise of Customer Advocacy

President Obama was elected in 2008 because he knew how to create and mobilize advocates. Through authentic community engagement, he was also able to raise half a billion dollars online in his 21-month campaign for the White House, dramatically ushering in a new digital era in presidential fundraising and advocacy.

In 2008, the Washington Post *provided insight into Obama's online operation based on the numbers: Three million supporters made a total of 6.5 million donations online, adding up to more than $500 million. Of those 6.5 million donations, 6 million were in increments of $100 or less. The average online donation was $80, and the average Obama supporter gave more than once.*

More than 13 million people provided their email addresses to the "Obama for America" campaign site and opted in to receive email messages about campaign news and events. They also created more than 2 million user profiles, wrote more than 400,000 blog posts, hosted more than 200,000 events, and established more than 45,000 volunteer groups throughout the United States. And just before Election Day, Obama supporters made more than 3 million phone calls to citizens advocating his election.

The number of Obama's Facebook fans or Twitter followers is irrelevant in this example. It wasn't the quantity or size of Obama's online community that helped him get elected. One of the primary reasons Obama was elected was his ability to inspire action. His supporters believed in his vision. They trusted in the "Change we can believe in" positioning statement. His supporters rallied behind him and told their friends, followers, co-workers, family members, and neighbors— and even called strangers every day for months to share his vision for the country. The volume of online conversation on Facebook, Twitter, and the entire social web sparked a groundswell of supporters for his vision. And the end result of this level of advocacy, on November 4, 2008, Barack Obama was elected President of the United States.

This is a valuable lesson and case study for business.

Most companies, products, and brands have advocates. An advocate is a person who loves or believes in something so much that he or she tells anyone and everyone about it. Advocates are influential and passionate, and they talk about the brands they care about even if no one is listening.

Advocates also play these roles:

- The brand's most satisfied customers

- Trusted sources of information

- Promoters and defenders of the brand

The term *influencer* is often used synonymously with *advocate*, but there is definitely a difference between the two. Advocates provoke action because of the level of trust they have with their circles of influence. They are trusted because they are authentic, and people trust their friends when seeking product advice. Advocates also play a significant role in consumers' purchasing behavior and are always willing to go the extra mile to answer questions about the brand or product. Companies need to think long term about creating programs specifically designed for their advocates.

An important distinction needs to be made here. The mere action of becoming a friend or fan and then following or just liking a brand inspires action. Imagine for a minute how a brand could put just a little effort in harnessing those potential relationships and invest in time, resources, energy, and creativity to build a program focusing on this relationship. Advocates are everywhere—they're dormant and just waiting to be activated.

The Difference Between Influencers and Advocates

Many companies don't understand the difference between an influencer and an advocate. Although some advocates can surely be influencers, not all influencers are advocates.

An influencer is someone with significant social capital—that is, influencers have a sizable audience on the social web. Many bloggers, analysts, and journalists are considered influencers because of their level of influence over the community reading their content. Many organizations create influencer outreach programs in an effort to reach an influencer's community by offering up products before they hit the market or giving the influencer insight into a product road-map. The relationship between a brand and its influencers is usually built upon incentives—for example, a brand sends an influencer an early model of a pre-released product, and the influencer writes about it on his or her blog.

Influencers may not necessarily care about the long-term health of the brands that consistently reach out to them to pitch a product. Instead, influencers generally have their own agendas, and the brand doesn't usually play a significant role. Influencers might have a short-term crush on a particular product or find it useful in some way, but they're being pitched all the time by companies looking to get some level of coverage. They certainly enjoy receiving free trials and new products before everyone else, and they'll very rarely say no when a company wants to send them a new shiny object.

The reality is, there are no guarantees when dealing with influencers. This situation is similar to working in media relations. Public relations teams pitch stories to journalists day after day; nine times out of ten, they get little to no results.

For influencers to stay influential within their community, they need to remain impartial to brands. Because they're often journalists, analysts, or bloggers, their readers expect them to stay above the marketing fray—or suffer the consequences of selling out to corporate America. The untold reality of many influencer outreach programs is that when a company stops sending influencers the latest products or stops flying them to the Consumer Electronics Show (CES) or other industry events, the conversation stops. Then the already infrequent tweets completely disappear, and the influencers might even criticize the brand because their ego was somehow compromised. With many influencer outreach programs, companies are merely renting the conversation, and the conversation isn't always authentic. If it was, companies wouldn't have to keep sending influencers new products to keep the conversation alive.

Advocates Love the Brand and Tell Others About It

Reciprocal altruism, as defined by Steve Knox, CEO of Proctor & Gamble's word-of-mouth division Tremor, is "[giving] to someone without any expectation of getting something in return."

This is a powerful statement that's not too common in business today. Companies need to adopt this thinking if they truly want to tap into the power of advocacy and create a groundswell of loyal and vocal customers. If they can take off their direct marketing hats and spend time valuing their customers, their customers will value them back—and they won't be afraid to tell others about it, either. Tapping into the emotional equity of customers will result in a long-term (and possibly profitable) relationship with them.

Advocates will still love the brand even when engaging in a one-sided conversation. Advocates will continue to praise the brand when it seems like the company isn't listening or responding to tweets or blog posts. They love the way a brand makes them feel, or look, or they like the value it brings to their lives. They may even love the brand because it feeds their own egos or makes a fashion statement. Whatever the reason, advocates are vocal, passionate, and unafraid to praise the brand (both online and offline). In some cases, advocates even defend the brand against criticism and negative feedback. And even though they might not have hundreds of Twitter followers, Facebook fans, or RSS subscribers, the conversation with advocates about the brand is always authentic. Why? Because they're being real and aren't trying to impress anyone.

> Advocates will continue to praise the brand when it seems like the company isn't listening or responding to tweets or blog posts.

Advocates can even serve as a powerful "virtual" sales force for any company—bringing in new customers; generating referrals; and spreading positive word of mouth on Facebook, Twitter, shopping sites, review sites, and more. Even better, this is all done merely through authentic conversations. As mentioned throughout this book, trust is key when making purchasing decisions. Consumers have a low level of trust in marketing communications, advertising, and corporate website content. They *do* trust people like themselves. Several credible resources, including the Edelman Trust Barometer and Forrester Research, have validated this numerous times.

The reality is that every company makes claims about the benefits of its product and services. But these claims become more meaningful and believable when existing customers are the ones saying it.

When a company can tap into advocacy, empower advocates to tell their stories, and then amplify those stories, the overall impact for business can be great for sales, awareness, or simply the brand story.

Nothing differentiates a company from its competitors more than positive customer reviews. Reviews can simply be conversations on Facebook and Twitter or official product reviews on third-party commerce websites such as Amazon. The competitive landscape is growing, and new products are coming to market everyday. No one can relate that message of product differentiation better than a company's existing customers.

Smart companies are tapping into the collective intelligence of their advocates and innovating their product offerings. Dell, Starbucks, and Lego are doing this successfully and changing the customer experience for millions of people. In doing so, they're also strengthening their bond with their advocates.

Measuring the Reach of Influencers and Advocates

When comparing one influencer to one advocate, the result is clear: Influencers reach more people with their messages. When an influencer speaks, his or her voice travels far across the Internet, through a series of retweets, Facebook shares, or blog posts.

Advocates, on the other hand, are just as influential, even though they don't have the same size community or the same reach that an influencer has. In a one-to-one comparison, the advocate loses the battle against the influencer, but this changes if a brand can create customer advocacy and make it the core of a social media marketing strategy. When a company can create an advocate program that taps into the emotions of their customers and empowers them to share their stories across the social web, the aggregate reach of all these conversations becomes exponential.

Companies should not completely ignore influencers, because they can certainly provide value. Influencers can play an important role in any social strategy when it comes to events, product launches, or quick coverage on an important initiative.

On the other hand, advocates provide much more business value because through their natural conversations, they are aiding and influencing their micro communities down and through the purchase funnel.

The "Advocate" Purchase Funnel

The traditional purchase funnel, described in Chapter 6, "Establishing a Measurement Philosophy," consists of five phases: awareness, consideration, preference, purchase, and advocacy. For years, marketers have spent millions of dollars and countless hours trying to understand which marketing tactics are the most effective at each phase of the funnel. They also spend time testing and hypothesizing about what type of messaging or advertising copy drives purchases within these phases. The traditional sales funnel is still important for marketers to understand and measure, but companies need to shift their focus to consider their advocates.

From an advocacy perspective, the purchase funnel is changing. It's no longer a funnel, coupled with a linear process of consumer buying patterns. Figure 10.1 illustrates that the advocate purchase funnel is more cyclical in nature; advocates are in the center, aiding and influencing their friends down the purchase funnel through natural conversations.

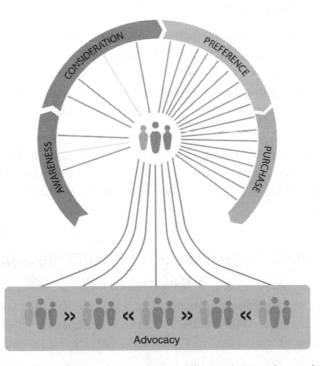

Figure 10.1 *Advocates are at the center of the purchase, aiding and influencing their circles of influence with purchase decisions.*

The advocate purchase funnel is important for many reasons. First, trust is key when making purchasing decisions. A 2009 Forrester Research study titled "How Customer Experience Drives Word of Mouth" found that 94 percent of consumers trust their friends when asking for product advice. This is compared to 34 percent for search engines, 28 percent for direct email, 18 percent for personal blogs, 18 percent for display advertising, and 16 percent for corporate blogs. Consumers commonly ask their friends for advice before they make any purchasing decisions.

Furthermore, people are more likely to recommend a brand or product after becoming a Facebook fan or Twitter follower, according to Chadwick Martin Bailey and iModerate Research Technologies. Their 2010 study titled "Consumers Engaged Via Social Media Are More Likely to Buy, Recommend" found that 60 percent of Facebook fans and 79 percent of Twitter followers were more likely to recommend those brands after becoming a fan or follower. In addition, an impressive 51 percent of Facebook fans and 67 percent of Twitter followers were more likely to buy the brands they followed or were a fan of.

The result of this data is clear: Advocates buy more when there is a mutually beneficial relationship with the brand, and that relationship usually exists on Facebook, Twitter, or both. And because advocates are trusted, they are influencing their own micro communities to buy as well. So in this scenario, it's a win–win for the consumer and the brand.

That said, companies need to focus on creating an advocacy program because that's what is going to get them "elected into office." Before they do so, however, they need to understand how consumers become advocates.

The Various Segments of Customer Advocacy

Similar to Forrester's Social Technographics Ladder of Participation, whereby consumers are segmented by social media usage and behavior, Zuberance, a company that specializes in identifying and empowering a brand's advocates, has classified advocates into similar groups:

- **General consumers**—Regularly read product reviews or stories, listen to podcasts, and read and engage in online forums.

- **Sharers**—Share their owns reviews (or reviews written by others), offers, videos, whitepapers, and event invitations; retweet "brand" tweets; and add tags to content such as photos and videos.

- **Creators**—Create their own reviews or stories, publish a blog, respond to other blogs and leave comments, actively tweet, and contribute to an online forum.

- **Power advocates**—Actively engage in the same behavior as the other segments, but also influence new customers down the purchase funnel through conversations, help organize events for the brand, give new ideas and offer feedback to the brand, and actively participate in formal customer advocacy groups.

Consumers follow a natural progression as they evolve from one type of advocate to the next. That is, as they interact and engage more with the brand (and establish a level of trust), they move from general consumers up the ladder to become sharers, creators, and then power advocates. This journey can be accelerated when a company opts to pay attention to customers and create formal advocacy programs.

How to Create a Customer Advocacy Program

Advocates congregate all over the Internet. They spend their time on Twitter, Facebook, blogs, forums, and other, smaller community sites. Before a company can find these advocates for its brand, it must be ready to scale its programs internally (budget, management, and a formalized documentation on how the program will function). Additionally, companies must ensure that the entire organization is fully vested in the program and ready to support it at all levels. When the program is in place, companies also need to be prepared to take action; merely listening and engaging with advocates isn't enough.

Organizational Readiness

Companies must not only commit to an advocacy program, but must also be ready to scale internally. Scale implies that organizations need to be prepared to allocate time, human capital, and budget to ensure the program has the right resources to grow. When a company has a large customer base, its programs will grow naturally over time, so it's important to have a plan of action that's supported by its company leaders. In many organizations, the marketing teams take "ownership" of customer advocacy programs and make them a part of the broader social media strategy. However, this requires tight collaboration with IT, customer support, and various product organizations.

Additionally, marketing also owns the advocate outreach and should develop a program that engages the advocates with fresh, relevant content. If applicable, IT must support the web infrastructure, assuming that the advocates will be invited to participate in an online branded community. The product groups will be involved if the advocacy program is centered on a specific product (such as Photoshop) instead of the corporate brand (such as Adobe).

Organizational readiness is the key in scaling a program such as this. Marketing, PR, legal, IT, customer support, and product groups all need to be involved when developing such programs. They should be a part of the planning process from the beginning and should also be key decision makers for issues that relate to their respective areas of responsibility. An effective advocacy program can have a positive impact on the entire organization through product innovation, feedback for customer support, word of mouth, and so on.

> An effective advocacy program can have a positive impact on the entire organization through product innovation, feedback for customer support, word of mouth, and so on.

After a company allocates its budget, puts a team in place to manage a program, and secures complete support from the organization, it can take the next step in finding its advocates.

Finding the Right Advocates

The next step in developing an advocacy program is to find the right advocates for the program. Only a few technologies can help companies achieve this. Simply Measured is a startup that builds social media measurement and reporting tools. Two products can help businesses of all sizes find advocates on Twitter and Facebook: RowFeeder and Export.ly.

RowFeeder performs keyword-based monitoring. It can track relevant topics, brand names, and trends, and create reports in Excel. It then can identify the most active participants and the most influential participants in any conversation relevant to the organization. By tracking a range of conversations over time, companies can build up deep knowledge about advocates that they can use to craft personal outreach.

Whereas RowFeeder provides a broad view of conversations, Export.ly narrows the scope. Export.ly exports and analyzes any Twitter account or Facebook fan page. This is useful in finding advocates within a company's owned media channels. Export.ly peels back the layers to learn about the audience, how influential they are, and how and when they are engaging.

Social media listening software, discussed in Chapter 2, "Surveying the Technology Supermarket," can also help find advocates beyond just Facebook and Twitter. By adding relevant brand- or industry-related search queries, most of these tools can find and report on the conversations happening around the web.

After collecting data and identifying advocates, companies have to determine the specifics of the program. Some companies invite advocates to private Facebook pages where they solicit their feedback, give advocates special offers or discounts, or offer advocates early exposure to new products. Other companies leverage LinkedIn and white-label community platforms such as Jive or Lithium.

Choosing the Right Advocate Platform

The last step is to find a platform that allows the company to communicate with its advocates and also allows the advocates to communicate with each other. Some companies create password-protected private communities where discussions are facilitated and managed. Other companies use existing platforms such as private LinkedIn groups and Facebook groups. In either case, it's imperative that these communities stay actively engaged with fresh content and discussion, to ensure active participation from the advocates. Examples can include weekly or monthly round-table discussions, feedback sessions, recognition programs, badges, and so on.

It's also important to give advocates insight into the business operations, provide product roadmaps, and extend invitations to events and to the corporate headquarters, provided that the advocates have signed a nondisclosure agreement (NDA). This level of engagement solidifies a long-term relationship between a brand and its advocates because the advocates feel valued. Chapter 1, "Human Capital, Evolved," highlighted a study that showed that 79 percent of consumers expect a brand to engage in social media. This level of engagement not only meets expectations, but exceeds them.

It's important to choose wisely when selecting a platform for an advocacy program—it's not easy to switch once the community is active and engaged. The advantage of creating a private community using a platform such as Jive is that it can be customized with widgets and badges, to essentially match the look and feel of the company brand identity. The disadvantage is that startup costs, development work, and monthly hosting fees add up. The alternative is to leverage existing platforms such as Facebook and LinkedIn groups, to build advocacy programs. The advantage of this approach is that it's a free solution, most people are already comfortable with the platform, and it wouldn't require people to create yet another profile. The disadvantage is that a company cannot customize anything and is essentially at the mercy of a third party.

Some companies are jumping into advocacy programs—not only finding advocates and inviting them to private communities, but also empowering them to share offers with their friends, write reviews, and tell their brand story to others through Facebook, Twitter, or social media platforms such as Zuberance.

Zuberance is one of the only hosted social marketing platforms available that enables companies to identify advocates, mobilize them to share content, and track metrics in real time (see Figure 10.2).

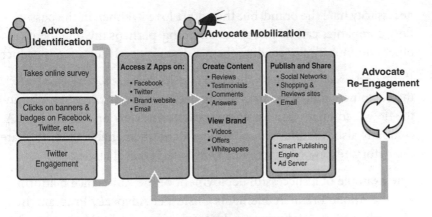

Figure 10.2   *The Zuberance user flow finds and mobilizes brand advocates to write reviews and share stories, and then tracks the program in real time.*

Zuberance has a three-step process for advocate programs that includes identification, mobilization, and sharing.

Advocate identification involves using a company's owned media properties, such as Facebook, Twitter, blogs, corporate website, and email database, to reach out to existing friends, fans, followers, and customers. Through a series of calls to action (using a banner advertisement on the corporate site, direct email, or a link in a Facebook status update) that simply says, "Hey, we want to hear from you!" or "Your feedback is valuable to us!", companies can find and segment their advocates. The call to action can be accompanied by a link to a branded page that asks the following question: "How likely are you to recommend my product?"

Similar to the Net Promoter Score management tool that's used to measure the loyalty of a company's customer relationships, users can choose between 0 and 10 to determine the next step in the flow. Consumers who choose 0–6 are considered detractors. Their feedback might not be exactly what a company wants to hear, but it's just as valuable. In this case, they can be easily routed to a page that captures their feedback, which can be stored and sent to the customer support department for follow-up.

Consumers who choose 7–8 are considered passives. It's impossible to determine how passives really feel about the brand. They might not necessarily hate the brand, but they don't love it, either. In the passive flow, companies can do just about anything, perhaps inviting them to other communities or sending them a discount code for a new product.

If the users select a 9 or 10, they are considered advocates. These are the customers that a company really needs to pay attention to. Within the flow, a company can ask them to write a review or share a story. A company also can offer a discount code and then enable them to share their story, review, or experience within their social circles.

One example of a successful deployment of the Zuberance platform was the Adobe Premiere Elements Customer Advocacy Program. In November 2010, Adobe approached Zuberance with a business problem. Very few Amazon reviews of the product were online, and they weren't very favorable. The product review average was about two out of five stars, and Adobe wanted to acquire more reviews before Black Friday.

Using the Zuberance platform, the Elements team identified advocates using direct email to their existing customer base. The team asked the question "How likely are you to recommend our product?" and then segmented the customers who selected 9 or 10. The next part of the user flow included asking the advocates if they would be willing to write a review on Amazon; many of them did.

The results speak for themselves. In early 2011, the product had more than 134 customer reviews, with an average star rating of four out of five stars.

Eloqua Case Study on Brand Advocacy

Joe Chernov is the vice president of content for Eloqua, which develops demand generation software, and also the co-chair of the Word of Mouth Marketing Association (WOMMA) member ethics panel. In 2010, Chernov decided to shift the focus of Eloqua's marketing efforts away from just growing the quantity of its followers on Facebook and Twitter, to instead learn more about its existing community and the nature of its followers.

The company conducts quarterly surveys of half of its more than 900 clients, capturing the Net Promoter Score (NPS) data on each client twice per year. Eloqua studies NPS trends across customer segments, products, user roles, renewals, and growth, and it cross-references patterns with changes in the company's product and service offerings. It develops, refines, or terminates programs depending on their impact on customer satisfaction.

In January 2010, Eloqua closely examined the patterns and conversational drivers in 500 tweets mentioning Eloqua, the dialogue within its 1,500-member Facebook fan page, and the discussion in its LinkedIn Groups. The company uncovered some compelling statistics.

Consumers who engage with Eloqua on social channels have a much higher NPS than the "average" customer. Overall, the NPS for customers who engage with the company is more than 450% higher than the NPS for the total customer base. Eloqua had assumed that the NPS for its Facebook fans would be the higher than for Twitter or LinkedIn. However, although Facebook fans registered a staggering 700% higher NPS score than the total client base, Twitter stole the show. A customer tweeting about Eloqua was nearly nine times as likely to be a brand promoter than the average user. Other data uncovered included the following:

- The company's blog was the number one trigger for customer tweets.

- Social CRM initiatives and customer support requests accounted for only 1 percent of all the customer tweets.

- Small to medium-sized business (SMB) clients were nearly 2.5 times as likely to create online content than enterprise clients.

- The more engaged the company was with a particular social network, the higher the NPS of the customers who were active in that community.

The key takeaway of this example is that when a company such as Eloqua actively engages on Facebook and Twitter in a two-way dialogue with its customers, those customers are more likely to recommend Eloqua to their friends, colleagues, and business partners.

Taking the Next Steps

Investing in an influencer outreach strategy is good for short-term promotional bursts. What company wouldn't want coverage on the home page of a powerful tech blog with millions of readers, fans, and followers?

Advocates, however, are passionate about the brand and don't require any incentives to tell others about it. A strong emotional connection drives them to share their experiences with their friends, their family members, and the communities they belong to. Advocates affect the purchase funnel in two ways. They buy the product or service repeatedly, and they aid and influence others with their purchase decisions. Organizations must recognize this early and create programs specifically for their advocates.

No matter who is driving the customer advocacy program, team members need to enlist support from other functional teams within the organization. Advocates need to be included and recognized by everyone, not just those in marketing. Besides, advocates might give excellent feedback on future product iterations, provide tips and advice to customer support, and even serve as beta testers for products that haven't yet been released to the general public. Advocacy programs are real-time focus groups, so the conversations extracted from them can prove insightful and actionable.

Listening to feedback from advocates is only half of the battle, of course. Companies need to be prepared to take action as well—within reason, of course. If advocates are vocal about wanting a new product feature and it makes smart business sense to build it, companies need to put their money where their mouth is and get it done. Otherwise, what's the point of having an advocate program?

Finding advocates on the social web takes time. An initial investment in tools that can help find those advocates is a wise decision. If a company already uses a social media listening platform, it can certainly use that as a starting point. In addition, companies can use tools such as RowFeeder and Export.ly to get more granular data.

Additionally, companies need to develop a content plan to keep their advocates engaged. This content plan can include monthly round-table conference calls, overviews of upcoming product releases, feedback sessions, or general discussions on how to improve certain processes, such as customer support.

Finally, companies that choose to create customer advocacy programs must stick with them for the long haul. The last thing a company

> For an organization to humanize its brand, it must first humanize its business operations, which is core to the social business evolution.

should do is abandon a community of advocates, because they're essentially the ones on the front lines of communication and telling their friends and families about their experiences. An advocacy program helps companies engage directly with their customers in a safe environment, and it also allows them to appear more human.

That said, for an organization to humanize its brand, it must first humanize its business operations, which is core to the social business evolution.

11

Ethical Bribe: Relevant Content Matters

It might sound like an oxymoron, but it really isn't. The ethical bribe is used by marketers to persuade consumers to take action or change opinions by sharing relevant content within social channels. The persuasion can include the repositioning of a product or brand, or it can help build (or protect) the reputation of a product, a brand, and in some cases, a CEO. It can be the introduction of a new product, new uses for an old product, a new innovation, or a phase-out of an old product.

A marketing campaign is nothing if not tactical. It typically asks the consumer to take action, such as joining a community, liking a Facebook fan page, following on Twitter, downloading a white paper, or subscribing to content. The ultimate call to action is to persuade consumers to purchase a product.

Every external piece of communication that a company creates and distributes to customers is a form of content. Web site copy, press releases, print collateral, whitepapers, advertising, search, the company logo, a piece of marketing collateral, and creative—it's all content. This form of content requires rounds of approvals from corporate marketing and legal to ensure that the material is honest, accurate, and "on message" within the brand guidelines. In most cases, this content alone, while ethical to its core, will not bribe anyone to do anything other than ignore it.

An ethical bribe, on the other hand, is designed to provoke consumers into action. It takes into consideration real discussions that are relevant to those who are interested. It reinforces the traditional marketing messages noted earlier. It's ethical because it's real, authentic, and transparent. The bribe, which may sound "unethical" to some, simply involves influencing and persuading those who are actually listening—and doing so in a way that's not deceptive.

> The bribe...simply involves influencing and persuading those who are actually listening—and doing so in a way that's not deceptive.

As the 2010 Edelman Trust Barometer reveals, consumers tend to find conversations with employees of a company and peers more credible than advertising, and they put more trust into experts and analysts than in CEOs.

An ethical bribe occurs when a company "humanizes" its marketing messages in an attempt to build a long-term relationship with consumers. However, paid media still plays an integral role for the ethical bribe to really make an impact. Why? Because paid media has the power to reach millions of people without much effort. To be truly successful, all outbound marketing from a company needs to be communicating the same message.

Figure 11.1 illustrates two customer journeys and the way each interacts with different forms of media (content) on the social web. This journey presents two challenges: one for consumers and one for brands. Consumers who live in the "stream"—that is, Twitter, the

Facebook newsfeed, FriendFeed, and Google Reader, for example—are inundated daily with hundreds of marketing messages. As a result, according to Brian Solis, consumers are creating attention dashboards to filter content that they're interested in following to stay abreast of what's going on in the social web and within their own microcommunities. Everything else is noise and usually ignored.

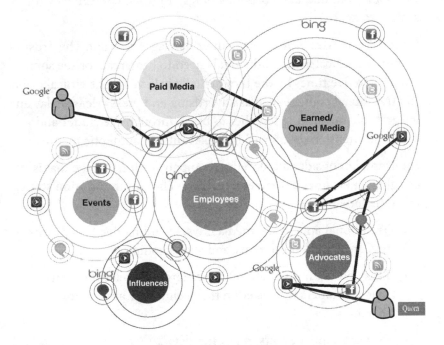

Figure 11.1   *The social customer's journey is dynamic and changes every day. He is creating filters to consume only the content that is relevant.*

Note that most consumers see only the content that is completely relevant to them at that precise moment. Figure 11.1 doesn't even take into consideration the traditional ways that many people communicate outside of the social web, such as through email, text messages, phone calls, and in-person conversations. The result of this "content chaos" that consumers go through each day is tunnel vision, with consumers filtering information and ignoring the content that they consider meaningless.

From a business perspective, the challenge is clear. If companies want their messages to be heard, understood, and believed, they have to fight for the consumer's attention. First, they have to be omnipresent on the social web and leverage multiple customer touch points with the same message. *Omnipresent* simply means that brands need to use paid media, such as display ads, search engine marketing, out-of-home advertising, broadcast, earned media (including influencer and advocate outreach programs), and owned media (including Twitter, Facebook, YouTube, and corporate blogs), to reach consumers with the same messages.

Second, businesses have to make their messages relevant. The Trust Barometer indicates that individuals need to hear, read, or see something up to five times before they actually believe it. The ethical bribe and traditional content such as advertising and press releases play an integral role in working together to break through the clutter and reach the attention dashboard in a relevant and authentic manner.

For example, consider a theoretical company called Orange that is bringing a new low-cost tablet to market. The communication strategy might include this:

- Traditional and online media buys, including display advertising, print and outdoor ads, and sponsorships

- Paid and natural search initiatives targeting relevant terms that consumers interested in this technology are already searching for

- Product launch events in key markets

- Aggressive engagement and community-building initiatives, including Twitter, Facebook, and blogs

- Influencer outreach programs

- Customer advocacy programs

- Employee engagement and amplification initiatives

A customer journey might look something like this. Jon, who is interested in purchasing a tablet, might first do a search in Google to see what's coming next. He clicks on an Orange paid advertisement, which takes him to the company's web site; he spends some time there reading about the features, specs, and cost. He clicks though to the corporate blog and subscribes to the RSS feed, to stay abreast of future product announcements and releases.

Later in the day, in his Facebook news feed, Jon notices a personal friend "liking" Orange's Facebook fan page. Curious, he clicks through and also "likes" the page to learn more; he reads through the Wall posts to see what others are saying. The next day, he asks his trusted community on Twitter whether anyone has purchased or knows anything about the new Orange Tablet. He gets a few responses and then notices several Orange employees responding to him on Twitter and answering his questions about the product. The next day, he receives an RSS notification via email from the Orange blog announcing a 25 percent promotion on the purchase of a new tablet. Finally convinced, he clicks through to the blog post, redeems the coupon code, and buys the new tablet.

Jon not only loves his new Orange tablet, but he is also super-impressed with the level of customer service he received throughout the process. He begins to talk about his experience online on Facebook and Twitter, and he might even blog about his experience. He also starts to evangelize the product on Twitter and answer specific product questions on Quora (a community where consumers can ask and answer questions) from people who are interested in the product. Orange recognizes that Jon is an advocate of the product and begins to pay more attention to him, sending him product swag, discounts, and accessories in appreciation of his support.

This is the ethical bribe.

In addition to having multiple content touchpoints to break through the clutter, companies need to be as relevant as possible when interacting with consumers on the social web. The ethical bribe relies on the fact that companies need to provide content that matters to the community. The net result of this content relevancy, and illustrated in the example of Orange and Jon, is true business value for the brand.

Relevant Content Creates Business Value

Content is the foundation upon which the entire social web exists. It involves everything—tweets, status updates, blog posts, online community discussions, videos, check-ins, and even Quora questions and answers. People read content, watch content, curate and aggregate content, listen to content, tweet content, retweet content, search for content, and like-vote-email-print-favorite-share-subscribe to content. Without social content, the Internet would be where it was almost 20 years ago.

But what's important is more than just content. Companies need to create the right content, at the right time, for the right person in the right channel.

When companies can achieve this level of content relevancy, they not only deepen community engagement and grow their existing communities, but they also create customer advocacy. This is one reason why social CRM is such a hot topic for business. A quick recap of Chapter 5, "In Response to the Social Customer: Social CRM," defines social CRM as coupling back-end, traditional CRM data with both external data from Twitter and Facebook and social listening data so that brands and marketers can provide a more relevant customer experience. The nature of that content influences the customer experience and is integral to the ethical bribe.

That being said, authentic, believable, and relevant content brings many benefits:

- Adds value to the conversation
- Happens as a result of listening and acting
- Positions the brand as a trusted advisor
- Is authentic and believable
- Builds trust with the community
- Increases the reach of branded messages
- Increases the "organic" search results

Adding all these together, relevant content drives true business value for the organization.

Relevant Content Adds Value to the Conversation

Many companies today aren't sure how to start engaging on the social web. One way to determine whether a conversation is happening about the brand—and where—is to conduct a conversation audit.

A conversation audit uses social listening software platforms such as Radian6 or Sysomos to scour the Web for brand- or product-related conversations. The data from an audit gives an organization insight into the following:

- Where the conversation is happening (Twitter, Facebook, forums, blogs)

- Nature of the conversation (sentiment, product, brand, or all)

- Share of voice in comparison to competitors or the general market category

- Influencer identification—their total reach, their community size, and where they spend most of their time online

- Competitive audit—competitors' community size, growth rate, and web traffic

The results of a conversation audit help organizations determine whether they can actually add value to the conversation going on around them. If the conversation is happening on Twitter and the sentiment revolves around complaints about the product, companies should jump into the conversation on Twitter to solve customer problems. If they aren't prepared to do this for any reason, they need to think long and hard about how they plan to engage on the social web. Merely saying "thank you" or just following disgruntled customers' Twitter accounts doesn't add value to the conversation and will most likely add fuel to the fire.

> The results of a conversation audit help organizations determine whether they can actually add value to the conversation going on around them.

That said, if the conversation is positive and results in several users praising the product, companies can say "thank you," retweet content, follow those users, and decide later how to engage them in a way that does add value. This could be creating formal advocacy programs, adding the users to specific Twitter lists, or inviting them to be a part of another community.

Companies can also add value to general inquiries about a product or brand. If customers need to know where to download the company's latest software driver, they can simply respond to the conversation with a link to the download page. Content like this not only adds value to the conversations, but it happens as a result of listening to the conversation.

Relevant Content Happens as a Result of Listening

A conversation audit identifies where exactly the conversations about a product or brand are happening. An audit also analyzes the nature and tone of the conversation. For example, if a company just launched a product, much of the conversation might involve recent purchases, likes or dislikes about the product, and in-depth product reviews. A conversation audit is a good first step, but ongoing listening helps brands understand how to engage—and where to engage—to add value to the conversations and become more relevant.

Many companies today are setting up command centers to accomplish this. They monitor the social web daily to identify customer service opportunities, address crisis-management issues, and get a more thorough understanding of the community at large. In early 2010, Gatorade created the Gatorade Mission Control Center inside its Chicago headquarters. It's a room that sits in the middle of the marketing department and resembles a scene from the sci-fi thriller, *Minority Report*; it calls to mind a war room for monitoring the brand in real-time across the entire social web.

Later in the year, Dell followed suit and launched its Social Media Listening Command Center. Dell is using Radian6 to power its command center and is tracking close to 22,000 topics daily related to the brand and its products.

Both Dell and Gatorade can use real-time data to solve customer problems and answer questions from existing customers and prospects. But the issue doesn't always have to relate to support or crisis management. Dell or Gatorade might well come across customers who are praising the brand. Amplifying those conversations through retweets or, in this case, saying "thank you," is a way to show the community that a company is listening and participating in both good and bad times. The listening data can also help companies understand exactly what matters to their customers.

If companies amplify the voices of customers and their messages, and basically "show them the love," customers will certainly reciprocate.

Relevant Content Positions the Brand as a Trusted Advisor

In the past, some companies have relied solely on press releases to launch products. Others have leaked product information to tech influencer blogs to leverage their reach, influence, and community size, as well as to create buzz. The problem with these two methods is that they result in a one-time communication opportunity. After all the hype and buzz dies down, a company has no way to communicate with the community again—until, of course, the next release hits the wires or the next blog post goes live (assuming that the third-party tech blog is willing to post it).

As companies today are getting more sophisticated, adopting governance models, and empowering their employees to blog and tweet, they've begun to rely on their owned media channels to share and leak information. An owned media channel is a company-owned community that controls the messaging, such as a corporate blog, a Facebook fan page, or a corporate Twitter account. The company can communicate directly with its community through these channels instead of having to go through a third party. And it makes sense that most consumers interested in a product or brand will want firsthand knowledge about a release date, future enhancements about a product or service, and other corporate communications.

As long as the messaging on a company's owned media channels is relevant, isn't inundated with sales propaganda, and delivers valuable information, the company can essentially position itself as a trusted advisor of content related to its own products and industry-related information. The key is to be authentic and trustworthy, with the end goal of being believable.

Relevant Content Is Authentic and Believable

One could question the authenticity of any politician, but during the 2008 presidential election, Barack Obama did something businesses can learn from. Not only was he authentic in the way he communicated, but his core message was believable. During his entire campaign, his message of "Change we can believe in" occupied every piece of media, every conversation, and every bumper sticker from California to New York. First, Obama was consistent with his messaging and emphasized the "change" point in every television appearance, speech, and interview. Second, the content of the message itself was very relevant for that time period. Most Americans wanted the war in Iraq to end and felt that a change in leadership would help facilitate that. Finally, Obama's supporters (his advocates) were sharing the same message with their own microcommunities in every channel and community they were a part of.

The lesson for business is that consumers today expect companies to be authentic. From a business perspective, content and messaging have to go beyond authenticity—they have to be believable. A company can truly be authentic in all its communication strategies, but if its content isn't relevant and doesn't add value, the community will not fully believe the message. The end result will be a huge disconnect and irrelevant messages that the community ignores.

> A company can truly be authentic in all its communication strategies, but if its content isn't relevant and doesn't add value, the community will not fully believe the message.

Building and fostering a healthy community, establishing trust, and becoming believable takes time before positive results emerge. Obama's message wasn't believed overnight; it took more than a year for voters, especially those in the middle, to learn to trust his vision for the country and vote for him. The same is true for business. A company cannot change its positioning overnight. It takes consistent and integrated messages to clearly communicate their new messaging throughout all media, especially within its social channels.

Relevant Content Builds Trust with the Community

The messenger of the content also plays an important role in building trust. As mentioned in the previous chapter, and according to the 2009 Forrester Research report, 94 percent of people trust their friends. The 2010 Edelman Trust Barometer also states that subject matter experts, employees of a company, and regular people are highly trusted and credible. These two data points and the general intuition of how people are influenced by their peers provides a clear lesson for business today.

Empowering employees to engage on the social web and share "branded" messages authentically is a natural way to build trust with the community. Equally important is identifying a company's advocates and empowering them to do the same. These two methods and the arsenal of other content (such as traditional marketing with display ads, search, print ads, and press releases) reinforce the company positioning and continue to foster trust within the community.

Building trust simply means that companies need to learn how to be human. A relationship between a brand and its customers is no different than a relationship between two really good friends in which listening, two-way communication, and some resulting action take place. However, before a company can learn to be human, it must learn how to humanize its business operations.

The entire first half of this book provides clear direction on how to humanize business processes and culture, and how to identify and empower employees to engage externally with customers. It first requires a shift in culture to truly make this happen effectively. Executive support, governance models, and training also play a vital role.

Chapter 10, "The Rise of Customer Advocacy," provides an in-depth look at customer advocacy and examines why advocates are trusted, their affect on the purchase funnel, and how to create advocate programs that work.

Building trust with a community requires keen listening skills. Without listening, a company might head into a conversation where it doesn't necessary belong.

Relevant Content Increases the Reach of Branded Messages

Most blogs and community-related websites use social bookmarking icons to enable their community members to more conveniently share branded content within their own personal networks. This is a widget that lets companies place customizable buttons on their blogs that let users share content that enables users to share content with the click of a button on Facebook, Twitter, Reddit, Digg, and email.

Consumers share content within their social networks when that content is valuable and relevant; the result of sharing is the increased reach of branded messages.

According to a 2010 study using AddThis data, users mainly share content on Facebook, which accounts for 44 percent of the total sharing volume using the tool. In 2009, this figure was only 33 percent. A similar study in 2010 from Chadwick Martin Bailey and iModerate Research Technologies found that close to half of consumers share content online at least once a week; the vast majority of content is shared through email (86%) and Facebook (49%).

Additionally, in 2010, Sysomos, a social media analytics platform, analyzed 1.2 billion tweets over a two-month period to identify what happens after a tweet is published. The research suggested that 30 percent of all tweets garner some form of reaction, in the form of replies or retweets. Although 30 percent might not seem like a huge number, it still accounts for more than 360 million tweets in just a two-month period.

> Consumers share content within their social networks when that content is valuable and relevant; the result of sharing is the increased reach of branded messages.

For example, assume that company A has 1,000 Twitter followers. Every time it shares a piece of content, its potential reach is 1,000. Of course, this number will naturally grow as the company acquires more followers. The reach of the messages will increase exponentially as more followers retweet the message. If one of the company's tweets gets retweeted 10 times and each of those followers has 1,000 followers, the total reach of that branded message would be the following:

1 tweet × 1,000 followers = 1,000

10 retweets × 1,000 followers = 10,000

1,000 + 10,000 = 11,000 total reach

An engaged community that finds value in content that is shared on Twitter is likely to share that content with its own microcommunities.

Content within blog posts operates in a similar fashion, just not as fast. When a company creates a relevant piece of content that is valuable to the community, the result is a waterfall of additional third-party blog posts referencing the original piece of content. So not only does the brand message spread organically, but it also results in inbound links, which are crucial to achieving high rankings in the organic search results.

Relevant Content Increases the "Organic" Search Results

It's a well-known fact that Google is nearly everyone's home page today. Millions search every day for information and click on links hoping to find the most relevant results possible. Many companies already spend millions of dollars with Google, paying for clicks and visibility within the sponsored search results. The main difference between sponsored search and organic search is that users can turn off sponsored search rather quickly. A company looking to gain visibility in the organic results may have to wait months to see any lift in the rankings. The key to achieving high organic search results is relevant content and inbound links; this makes the sum and quality of links pointing back to a company's website or blog very important.

Another differentiator between paid and organic search is that organic search results cannot be bought. Many companies attempt to manipulate Google in an effort to increase their visibility, but it's a huge risk that can get their web site banned from the search results if they're caught.

When companies are developing the content they plan to share on Twitter, Facebook, and corporate blogs, it's good practice to first understand what people are searching for in Google. Along with listening and monitoring on the social web, this will help companies guide their content planning.

Consider a quick illustration. The Google Keyword tool is a free online tool that identifies relevant keywords and their corresponding search volume. For example, a quick search for "phone service" yields the following results:

- "Phone service" is searched for approximately a million times per month in Google.

- "Long distance phone service" is searched for approximately 10,000 times per month in Google.

- "Residential phone service" is searched for approximately 8,000 times per month in Google.

Volume is important to consider because higher-searched terms are more difficult to attain high rankings for, simply because of the competition. Most telecommunication companies probably want to rank number one in Google for "phone service" because of how many people are searching for it each month. In this example, it would certainly make sense for a company to write a blog post titled something like "Learn more about our residential phone service" and then share it on Facebook and Twitter. Eventually, Google will index that blog post and it will appear in the search results when users search for "residential phone service."

The end result of creating relevant content that exactly matches what consumers are searching for can result in engagement, community growth, and search engine visibility.

Taking the Next Steps

Two types of content are discussed in this chapter: proactive content and reactive content.

Proactive content considers all outbound engagement and includes the sharing and distribution of brand-related messages on corporate blogs, Twitter, Facebook, YouTube, and other owned media properties. Proactive content can include product- or company-related announcements, industry perspectives, contest management, and other promotions.

For proactive content to be relevant and impactful, it's important to have a content strategy. The first step in creating a content strategy is to listen to the external nature of the conversation using social media listening platforms. This strategy also includes listening internally to product organizations, marketing, and public relations; and understanding the product road map, upcoming events, and announcements that might be relevant to the community.

The second step involves content planning. The findings from listening both externally and internally will help craft an editorial calendar encompassing each of the company's owned media properties, including Facebook, Twitter, YouTube, and corporate blogs. Some companies create just weekly or biweekly editorial calendars. However, it's good practice to also maintain a six-month thematic calendar that documents and includes upcoming events, holidays, product launches, and other topics of interest to customers.

The third step is content creation. This can include writing blog posts with corresponding tweets and Facebook status updates. It may also include creating video content, tutorials, and other programming ideas.

The fourth step is the actual execution. The engagement can include informing and connecting with community members, responding to comments and tweets, answering questions, providing context to and around a topic, and also collaborating with or co-creating content with the community.

The last step in the content strategy is measuring the effectiveness of the engagement. It's important to understand which types of content drive the most engagement in terms of retweets, comments, likes, shares, page views, and impressions. With insights into the analytics, companies can create content that the community finds most relevant. This deepens community engagement and increases the reach of branded messages.

Reactive content happens as a result of listening to conversations on the social web and responding when relevant. It can certainly include responding to comments on corporate blogs, Twitter, and Facebook, but it can also entail leaving comments on third-party blog posts. Usually, reactive content deals with customer support issues, crisis communications, responses to critical comments, and corrections to faulty information.

It's important for companies to have a crisis communication plan and be prepared to act quickly if they have to. In this situation, it's imperative to be proactive instead of reactive because time will be of the essence. If a company isn't prepared to act in a timely fashion, a potential crisis might only worsen.

Setting up a command center is ideal for monitoring brand-related conversations. However, in most cases, much of the monitoring will come from a community manager, a support team member, or an employee who is monitoring Twitter. In any case, having a process for flagging potential support issues and ensuring that the customer problem is solved is a priority. The good news is that many of the social media listening platforms are equipped with workflow-management systems that can classify posts, tag them, and route them to team members for follow-up.

> Search engine optimization teams... need a clear understanding of what people are searching for that relates to the company, brand, products, or industry.

When a company is looking to launch a new blog or community platform, it must enable community members to share and add content to Facebook, Twitter, Digg, Reddit, and other social aggregators or bookmarking sites as conveniently as possible. Additionally, adding the functionality of emailing content to friends is important because most people share social content online in this way.

Finally, it's important for anyone responsible for outbound engagement to partner with internal search engine optimization teams. They need a clear understanding of what people are searching for that relates to the company, brand, products, or industry. These insights will help drive future editorial, in an attempt to be more relevant, increase engagement, and grow the community.

The ethical bribe is a way to influence the community in some way to change the perception of a brand, reposition the company, grow the community, increase engagement, and sell products. For the ethical bribe to be effective, companies need to consider the amount of content people consume every day, their own content, and how content can be used to influence, inform, and educate across all media and communication channels.

12

Social Businesses in the Real World: EMC and Intel

This book serves as a playbook for companies that want to evolve into fully operational and collaborative social businesses. In a perfect world, company leaders realize early on that they need to change the way they do business to stay competitive, innovate, and ultimately address the dynamic nature of the social customer. The focus is to get the internal house in order first and address issues such as organizational culture, silos, and models; then the company adopts social media best practices for technology, governance, training, collaboration and processes, and workflows. When this is almost complete, the focus naturally shifts to addressing external engagement strategies for interacting with the social customer.

To reiterate, an organization cannot effectively engage with customers unless its employees can effectively engage internally with each other first.

However, the reality is that every organization is different. Each company's journey is dynamic; it will change course multiple times as the market moves, leadership changes, culture dynamics shift, and new organizational models are designed. Some companies might already have an open, collaborative organization and simply face technology challenges that prohibit them from getting to the next step. For others, technology might not be the challenge; they might still be operating in the old-school "command and control" mindset and are afraid to change. The nature of social business requires a company to have all its operations working together collaboratively at all times. When a process is broken or internal communication fails, the entire organization can suffer the repercussions. Worse, the social customer will also suffer—and will surely tell others about it.

> An organization cannot effectively engage with its customers unless its employees can effectively engage with each other first.

Many companies today struggle with moving their organizations through this evolution and are seeking answers. Either they can't persuade their managers and executives to change or their organization might be too big for them to make an impact. Maybe they just can't afford technology solutions that will allow them to collaborate. Or maybe the organization already has multiple social media initiatives but they're all working in silos.

Many companies have successfully navigated the transition to a social business and faced these thorny issues head on. Two tech companies, EMC and Intel, are notable because they successfully operationalized social media internally.

EMC is unique because it focused internally first, creating a fully collaborative, social organization. Next, EMC unleashed its employees to engage externally with customers. The results speak for themselves. Several hundred EMC employees engage on Twitter, which has resulted in fully collaborative internal and external communities where business and technology conversations are happening daily.

Intel's evolution was different yet just as effective. It started as a grass-roots effort more than 10 years ago, when technology experts and IT managers were engaging in forums and chat rooms, talking shop with other IT managers. Today Intel has a Social Media Center of Excellence that helps drive governance and training across the organization. It has fully embraced social media as a viable channel to engage with customers and partners. Intel's internal culture and organizational models allow the company to empower employees, integrate social with all other media, and scale its technology platforms as the business grows.

The following case studies were conducted via interviews with EMC's Director of Social Engagement, Len Devanna, and Intel's social media strategist, Bryan Rhoads.

EMC's Social Business Evolution

EMC is a business-to-business (B2B) company that develops, delivers, and supports information infrastructure and virtual infrastructure hardware, software, and services. It is a Financial Times Global 500, Fortune 500, and S&P 500 company with offices globally and head-quarters in Massachusetts.

EMC has effectively reinvented itself during the past decade. In 2000, EMC held the title as leading provider of enterprise storage systems. By 2010, EMC not only retained that title, but also became the fifth-largest software provider in the industry.

This growth was driven organically but also through an aggressive acquisition strategy: EMC acquired more than 50 companies between 2002 and 2008. With each acquisition came a new group of employees, a new culture, and a new market. Although such growth is wrought with complexity, it has proven to be extremely rewarding to EMC and its customers. At the same time, acquisitions naturally force an organization to evolve its culture. This dynamic is challenging for thriving organizations that want to become a social business because one culture must become multiple cultures. Each new acquisition has forced EMC to learn and adapt.

The Early Days of Social Media

EMC had approximately 46,000 global employees in 2010 and many diverse product offerings and business units conducting operations across the globe. As with similar-sized companies, a strong ecosystem of partners, customers, suppliers, and other stakeholders plays an integral part within the overall business strategy. As with any company of any size and complexity, fluid communications across stakeholders is key.

In mid-2007, EMC formally began its journey toward becoming a social business and a fully engaged enterprise. At the same time, it faced the realities of explosive growth, cultural integration for several acquisitions, and a rapidly evolving digital landscape. EMC recognized that it had an opportunity to begin engaging externally with partners and customers, but the organization wasn't ready. No one was using social media internally or externally, so it faced a severe learning curve. Starting at ground zero was the only option.

A small and agile team in the corporate communications department assembled and began to plan for EMC's expansion into social media. The team opted not to treat this like a traditional project with a lengthy business case, goals and objectives, large investment ask, and numerous approvals from senior management.

"In the spirit of the evolution of 2.0, we opted to work outside the confines of traditional thinking and take a more stealth approach," says Len Devanna, Director of Social Engagement.

Among the first major steps in EMC's evolution into a social business was the need to begin conversations with a broader audience internally, to explore the opportunities to engage externally. EMC's new team built an internal community in just a few days, using the freeware platform Drupal. The length of time between conception and launch of this initial community was a matter of days, not weeks or months, a timetable largely unheard of in an enterprise the size of EMC.

Next, the team invited a larger, more diverse group of employees who were excited about EMC products and customers to participate in the community. They focused on figuring out how to operationalize social media internally and change the culture at the same time. Simply inviting employees to be more open and transparent within the community and soliciting feedback contributed significantly to the culture change. The first conversation that seeded the subsequent evolution of EMC into a social business was, "What are the opportunities afforded to EMC and its customers via social media?"

As time progressed and conversations blossomed, the adoption and use of this new community grew exponentially.

EMC Experiences Strong Internal Community Growth

The internal conversation at EMC went viral quickly. A groundswell effect arose within the company, and an appetite emerged for new collaborative capabilities, discussions, and ideas. This sent a strong message to senior management. If a zero-dollar investment can generate such a high degree of collaboration and employee engagement, what would happen if EMC put real energy, time, budget, and planning into the evolution of this new real time communications shift?

EMC quickly outgrew its experimental community and needed to move on to something more robust with a broader set of capabilities and functionality. The existing platform could not scale with the number of employees using it to create profiles and join the conversation.

EMC's initial investment into its social business evolution was extremely small, considering the impact it would have (thousands of dollars, as opposed to tens of thousands). Needing to move beyond the freeware platform, EMC chose an emerging vendor in the community space, Jive, but opted to purchase only a small number of licenses as the initial investment. The plan was to scale investment and adoption slowly, with hopes that the growth of the community and the conversations taking place would make the case for subsequent and much bigger investment ask. In the proceeding months, that would prove to be an effective strategy.

It quickly became apparent that the interesting story was not necessarily the tools or the platforms, but rather the cultural and behavioral changes that were taking place as a result of having a community offering. The conversations within the community revolved around EMC's business strategy, internal policies, and ways to communicate more effectively. Employees were also having personal conversations.

This internal community came to be known as EMC|ONE, with ONE serving as an acronym for the Online Network of EMCers.

The impact and influence of the community quickly became clear when executive management proposed a new mobile phone policy within EMC|ONE. The community backlash against this policy was overwhelming, to say the least. It was one of the first times that most employees rallied together to push back publicly against a new policy proposed by management. As a result, all levels of the company came together to collaborate on a new mobile policy that worked for everyone across the organization.

EMC's Decision to Start Internally First

Several fundamental decisions were made early on, and they turned into guiding principles for EMC's transformation into a social business. The most important was building a high degree of employee proficiency before focusing on external audiences.

EMC wanted to focus on the skills and behaviors within the organization before going outside the comforts of the corporate firewall. EMC also wanted to learn the nuances of social media—the etiquette, the challenges, and also the opportunities. In a sense, the social media team wanted to focus on the *social* side of social media.

Because this community was started internally, EMC was able to engrain social media into the fabric of employees' daily workflows. It was an internal sandbox where EMC employees could test the waters, experiment, and learn the tools; at the same time, they learned how to use these behaviors to do their jobs more effectively.

By this time, EMC|ONE consisted of a small yet passionate and influential group of employees from every region. These early adopters of social media were critical to the growth, influence, and adoption of the community across EMC. They became the social champions, helping to oversee the direction and strategy of EMC|ONE while also serving as evangelists throughout the business, creating excitement and helping to expand the community by encouraging their coworkers to give it a try.

Another major component to EMC's early strategy was to resist the desire to have closed conversations. They found that, in most instances, employees were more comfortable having conversations in small groups than in public forums, not unlike public speaking. They knew that if they encouraged this dynamic, they would find themselves trapped with hundreds of closed-off communities and conversations; the result would be a lack of transparency and openness.

Since the beginning of this evolution, EMC embraced a policy of openness. Knowing that EMC|ONE was available only to employees, the team pushed back on requests for private spaces, asking what information was so sensitive that peer employees could not be privy to it. Although some initial resistance to this arose in the early days, the policy helped EMC|ONE avoid becoming a siloed organization and go beyond just community discussions. With all the recent acquisitions and blending of cultures and behaviors, this was a significant effort.

"We've repeatedly seen value in employees from across the globe participating in discussions from other business units or geographies on a variety of different topics," says Devanna.

Interestingly, not only did this policy contribute to the collaboration on EMC|ONE, but EMC as a company also became an organization of openness willing to communicate publicly about important topics.

As with any new technology or business initiative, there is always a desire for control, by either IT, operations, or executive management. Early on, many discussions revolved around governance, with some even suggesting that every conversation would have to be moderated and approved before publishing. Instead, EMC opted to take a lightweight governance approach, influenced by the fact that the conversation was happening behind the firewall. EMC's position was clear. Community members were also employees. They're adults, paid by EMC, and any malicious individual or employee could do as much damage via traditional tools such as email as they could in a closed community. EMC was careful not to confuse governance with security; even though the conversations were open, the underlying technology was secured by the IT department.

EMC opted to embrace a basic approach of trust. Instead of tightly controlling or moderating content, the company focused on a basic strategy of education and empowerment. EMC used traditional techniques such as "lunch and learns" to teach employees why social media was important to them as individuals and to EMC as a brand. Employees were also trained to leverage tools such as EMC|ONE to work more seamlessly across the organization.

> Instead of tightly controlling or moderating content, EMC focused on a basic strategy of education and empowerment.

The conversations in EMC|ONE began to grow exponentially. For example, many employees started using EMC|ONE as a way to share information using the blogging functionality in Jive. They used the internal platform to experiment and find their online voices in a safe environment with other community members.

EMC also created a watercooler space within EMC|ONE, to coax employees who were not familiar with social media or communities in general into participating. The Watercooler was a place where employees could talk about their cats, their cars, or whatever they were interested in; it was designed to help them take that first step into real-time community engagement. This stepping stone helped employees feel comfortable communicating in an open environment, and it equipped them with the know-how in a safe environment.

In addition, community spaces such as EMC's Social Media Club began to resonate, furthering the discussion around the opportunities for EMC in the external social landscape. Then a wiki was created that described the company's activity on Twitter and identified conversational gaps on the social web. According to Devanna, "The organic growth that was realized from the inside-out approach made it extremely easy to begin taking the conversation outside the firewall and engaging new audiences."

Today more than 15,000 employees from around the world are engaging in conversations via EMC|ONE. The communities are vibrant and open, and many of the company's employees have become proficient at using social media.

EMC Opens Up the Corporate Firewall

In January 2009, with a solid understanding of community building and social engagement, EMC launched the ECN, or the EMC Community Network. Similar to EMC|ONE, the ECN brought an external community to EMC's customers, partners, suppliers, and other audiences, such as analysts, journalists, and influencers.

"The ECN is helping us realize a completely new model of co-innovation. It's helping us break down traditional corporate barriers and further put our customers at the center of our business," says Devanna.

Today the ECN has a community of more than a quarter-million members. Using the channel, EMC exposes prerelease products for input, collaborates with customers to help them solve their IT challenges, and provides a forum for customers to easily access EMC employees, engineers, and customer support teams. The community is broken down by the following topics:

- Product- and solution-specific forums
- Support-related forums
- EMC labs
- Developer programs

Additionally, to support product launches, initiatives, and events, EMC creates a social activation kit, which is a wiki document that helps employees who participate externally understand the following components:

- Key supporting messages
- Supporting content, including video assets, blog posts, and press releases
- Customer-shortened links, for tracking purposes
- Hashtags

The social activation kit is used for every external engagement opportunity that is relevant to EMC's customers and partners.

Through the ECN, EMC employees work with customers to solve important issues and have relevant conversations with the community. As a result, EMC's social footprint is growing.

EMC's Social Footprint

In 2009, EMC was ranked the 14th most socially savvy brand by NetProspex, a company that uses the power of crowdsourcing techniques to analyze social activity and engagement. From page views on the EMC Community Network to its aggregate reach on Twitter, EMC registers between 10 million and 20 million social impressions per month.

Although reach is the easiest measure, EMC puts far more value in its level of engagement with customers and partners. Specifically, the company is constantly measuring Key Performance Indicators (KPIs) at the engagement mix of EMC versus non-EMC conversations, ensuring that the social media team is actively participating and providing constant business value to its audience. A few KPIs used to measure the team's effectiveness include the following:

- Employee versus nonemployee engagement
- Frequency of visits to community properties (return visitors, unique visitors, page views, and so on)
- Time between questions posted and answered
- Net-promoter and advocacy sentiment

EMC's community is thriving; in-depth technology conversations on a variety of topics between employees, customers, and partners are the norm within the ECN. The company's Twitter activity also shows high levels of engagement, including consistent retweets and @mentions. In addition, EMC often shares links to partner/customer content that add value to the conversation.

EMC's Organizational Model and Governance

In 2010, EMC reorganized its social media team, moving it from the web team to the corporate communications team and aligning it with the likes of public and analyst relations. This reorganization was designed to help evolve EMC's overall communications model while ensuring that social media and community building was a core component of its emerging communications strategy.

The social media team actively encourages employees from other EMC organizations and geographies to participate in the social web. It has created simple social media guidelines that help employees get started, based on a few key principles:

- Use common sense.
- Be transparent.
- Add value.

To ensure consistency, the team manages a wiki of EMC "voices," a landing destination where social media is discussed in detail. The team also covers what area of expertise each employee should talk about externally with customers. In other words, the team encourages broad participation but also asks that EMC employees respect the basic principles—be transparent, add value, use common sense—and keep a keen eye on the customer experience.

EMC believes that social media should be a core part of everyone's job and has strongly embraced a mantra of "Educate, enable, and scale" with regard to its employee base. The social media team has taken this vision and deployed several training courses designed to help educate employees on the importance of community engagement and how to use tools such as Twitter and Facebook.

Another organization that exemplifies attributes of a social business is Silicon Valley chip maker Intel Corporation.

Intel's Social Business Evolution

Ever since the Intel Inside campaign in 1991, Intel has had a steady cadence of digital communications. Intel was an early adopter of using the web as a business tool, launching corporate web sites as early as

1995. Intel's online presence quickly grew to include product support and channel and developer partners.

In the late 1990s, Intel.com—and, specifically, Intel's Customer Support site—offered a wide array of early social technologies, such as forums and message boards. The Intel Architecture Labs created nascent Internet Phones and video codecs. To support these online efforts, the teams experimented with early virtual worlds such as thepalace.com and a 2-D virtual world called the Intel Boardwalk.

The 2000s saw the continued development and experimentation of Intel's digital offerings. Of note were academic research projects with schools such as the MIT Sloan School of Management. A four-year online project named Web Trust launched in 2001.

Today Intel is a fully engaged social business. Internally, employees are communicating and collaborating across business units, job functions, and geographies. Employees at all levels also are empowered to engage externally on behalf of the brand. The Social Media Center of Excellence (SM COE) is helping to streamline communications and create process and governance models that address the use of social media externally.

The company is using social technologies such as Jive and Microsoft SharePoint Intel to create and manage internal employee communities that are an active part of their employee communications strategy. In particular, Intel's internal Planet Blue employee social networking plat-form has become a critical collaboration asset for more than 90,000 employees around the world.

Externally, Intel has a significant presence on Twitter, YouTube, Facebook, corporate blogs, and communities. Company leaders, mar-keting teams, and various business units have fully embraced social media as a viable channel to communicate with customers, suppliers, partners, and, in some instances, competitors.

The Early Days of Social Media at Intel

In many respects, Intel followed a classic social media adoption cycle. In 2005, web and digital innovation happened at the edges, with smaller business units and grassroots bloggers using social media to communicate externally.

These early adopters were actively engaged in social media to address customers' needs and solve business problems. One of the first teams to engage externally was Intel's software developer group. The team understood early on that the target audiences were also early adopters of social technologies such as blogs and communities. After initial pilot blogs started by employees, the group formally created the Intel Software Network (ISN); this is now a thriving community where deep technology conversations are happening daily between Intel and its partners.

After the early adopters demonstrated success in building communities, more formalized pilots followed. In 2006, Intel's social media strategist, Bryan Rhoads, launched the first official corporate blog focusing on the IT audience. Intel's IT@Intel blog was the first of many multiauthor blog channels that Intel developed to connect with audiences who were using social media to communicate and collaborate. That same year, it won a "Best in Class" audit award from industry web analysts and garnered accolades from the tech press.

"The IT@Intel blog was the perfect pilot candidate for launching our blog platform. We built a pilot blog for our own Intel IT managers and had them communicating on topics that were important to their peers in the industry and in IT—real topics like information security, wireless network management, and even information overload. These topics and others are universal to the IT audience and fulfilled a peer-to-peer communications requirement to keep them authentic and interesting," says Rhoads.

In 2006, social media was decentralized and essentially uncoordinated among teams across Intel. Intel had an early social media advocacy group called the Blog Ambassadors, made up of enthusiast employees whose mission was to promote social technologies at Intel. But beyond this volunteer group, Intel had no central strategy or governance.

Senior management also realized the potential risk associated with the rise of employees blogging without any formal guidelines, process, or training in place.

With the rise of employee involvement and the growing need to connect with audiences, Intel management realized that the company required a deliberate and integrated approach to social media. Senior management also realized the potential risk associated with the rise of employees blogging without any formal guidelines, process, or training. In 2008, Intel created the Social Media Center of Excellence to serve as a central advisory and strategy team and to move the company forward as a social business and address many of the governance issues.

The Establishment of the Social Media Center of Excellence

The Intel Social Media Center of Excellence (SM COE) was formed to bring social media at Intel to the next level. A main goal was to learn from the employees who were already actively engaged with Intel customers within social channels and to make them part of the planning process. This was a strategic decision meant to collaborate with employees who already had significant experience and influence across the social web. Additionally, their involvement was the first step toward scaling social media throughout Intel's global employee base.

The SM COE is also responsible for crafting the global social media strategy and marketing integration. The team recommends and establishes social media integration techniques into more traditional and digital marketing, such as paid media, online, print, and even broadcast/TV globally.

The SM COE is also responsible for training employees at all levels in digital communications and social media. Social media participation is open to all employees, and Intel requires training to participate on behalf of the brand and Intel. A 30-minute on-demand video course certifies employees as Intel social media practitioners (SMPs); it covers Intel's global social media strategy, legal cautions, guidelines, and case studies of successful and not-so-successful social media programs.

The SM COE is also responsible for driving collaboration among all SMPs and ensuring that sharing best practices is top-of-mind for everyone participating in social media. Part of this scale includes building a collaborative employee SMP community for knowledge sharing, social coordination, and crisis management. The SM COE fosters the SMP community and has created email distribution lists, social media alerts and announcements, and newsletters to keep Intel's growing army of SMPs abreast of the latest trends in social and emerging media.

Finally, Intel's SM COE is responsible for establishing measurement and metrics frameworks and managing social listening tools. Empowering Intel's SMPs and business units with measurement strategies and techniques has been critical to the growth of social media adoption as a business and marketing communications tool.

One of Intel's most recognized successes in the social media industry was publishing its social media guidelines externally (you can find it at www.intel.com/sites/sitewide/en_us/social-media.htm) near the end of 2008. These guidelines were made public in more than 30 languages. Creating the social media guidelines was a collaborative effort between the SM COE, the early adopter employees, and internal advocacy groups.

"It was very much like crafting a piece of legislation as we included those employees who had been at the forefront of social media at Intel. Each employee stakeholder was representing their distinct role, business unit, and customer base. The goal was to craft a democratic document that accounted for the employee's desire to utilize social tools in their jobs and also addressed management's concerns around risk mitigation and the potential 'oversharing' of proprietary information. By leveraging the enthusiasts, we ensured that the tone was transparent in accordance with social media standards and that it would be met with widespread adoption from employees," says Rhoads.

Intel's social media guidelines have served as an industry example and been emulated by other Fortune 500 companies, private firms, and even some state and local governments. The guidelines are written in plain language and avoid heavy legal jargon. Some main points of the policy include these:

- Stick to your area of expertise and provide unique, individual perspectives on what's going on at Intel and in the world.

- Post meaningful, respectful comments—in other words, no spam and no remarks that are off-topic or offensive.

- Always pause and think before posting. That said, reply to comments in a timely manner, when a response is appropriate.

- Respect proprietary information and content, as well as confidentiality.

The guidelines serve as rules of engagement for Intel SMPs and even agencies or third parties representing Intel or managing social media programs. These same guidelines serve as the backbone for the overall SMP training and include topic credos such as "Write what you know, and know what you write," "Perception is reality," and "If it gives you pause, take a pause." These all remind authors to be mindful of their content at all times.

Intel also established its corporate-wide moderation policy with the same spirit of openness and transparency. The policy asks all participants to follow three memorable principles: "The Good, the Bad, but not the Ugly." The guidelines state, "If the content is positive or negative and in context to the conversation, then we approve the content, regardless of whether it's favorable or unfavorable to Intel. But if the content is ugly, offensive, denigrating, and completely out of context, then we reject the content."

Intel Social Media Footprint Focuses on Employees

After Intel employees complete the main social media training course, called "Digital IQ 500," they are considered official SMPs. Intel SMPs can participate on behalf of Intel in all forms of social media. More than 1,600 SMPs represent Intel from all business unities, geographies, and levels of management.

That number of 1,600 SMPs equates to several tens of millions in effective and potential reach of Intel messages. These practitioners are active on all major social networks around the globe, from Facebook to RenRen, from vKontakte to Twitter. This level of engagement by Intel employees has resulted in huge increases in community growth. As of April 2011, Intel's Facebook page had more than 1 million fans and 40,000 followers on Twitter.

Social Media Ownership of Intel

The Social Media Center of Excellence was created to help steer and guide the ship. Sitting within Intel's Corporate Marketing Group, the team is situated in Marketing Strategy and works closely with the web marketing team, the public relations department, and creative and brand teams. They work with all the geographies, business groups, and product teams to develop strategies, social properties, and tactics for the entire marketing and communications mix at Intel.

However, each team and group at Intel is responsible for its own execution and microstrategies relevant to its mission, business goals, and geography. Individuals and teams coordinate and develop their own social assets and communications. The teams themselves activate and integrate social media into specific campaigns, web properties, and media.

Conclusion

Many organizations today spend a lot of time, resources, and financial investment trying to understand the social landscape and engaging externally with their customers and prospects. They are on a quest to become a social brand. They are investing in Facebook applications, branded communities, and blogs; many are using online monitoring solutions to listen to what people are saying about the brand. From this perspective, many companies today are doing a decent job.

Friends, fans, and followers are important, yes. And brands increase their social equity by engaging in two-way dialogue with their constituency, yes. And transparency is key to these external engagements, yes. But while many organizations are trying desperately to humanize their brand, they are failing to understand that they need to humanize their business first.

And therein lies the business challenge. As the use of Facebook, Twitter, and other social applications grew and as the influence of the social customer became apparent, companies of all sizes and in every division began to join the conversation. Not only did customers expect it, but social influencers enjoyed playing Monday morning quarterback and criticizing brands for every action and inaction.

And companies listened. Today organizations are aggressively hiring community managers and social strategists, allocating budgets to social media, hiring agencies, and creating engagement strategies. They are doing everything a "good" social brand should be doing.

But this book is not about social brands. It's about an organization's natural (sometimes forced) evolution into a social business. A social business deals with the internal transformation of an organization and addresses key factors such as organizational models, culture, internal communications, collaboration, governance, training, employee activation, global and technology expansion, team dynamics, and measurement philosophy.

For companies to do this effectively, they have to get smarter; acquire new technologies, intelligence, and talent; and become more open and transparent. They have to establish processes and governance models that protect the organization yet empower employees. They have to change the way they do business, and that starts with the people of the organization.

An organization that uses social media to engage externally with customers is a social brand, not necessarily a social business. There's a huge difference.

From the outside looking in, most wouldn't recognize or understand the challenges that social media has created in the enterprise. The anarchy, conflict, confusion, lack of communication and collaboration, and organizational silos that exist behind the firewall are not visible. These challenges make the process of becoming an effective social brand much more difficult and less effective. So for some organizations, this quest to become a social brand and a social business is one of a simultaneous effort.

The key takeaway of this book is that organizations cannot and will not have effective, external conversations with consumers unless they can have effective internal conversations first. And much more than internal conversations, conference calls, and a collaboration forum are needed. For this evolution to take place, organizations need to adopt social behaviors in every aspect of their business operations.

Index

U

V

W

Y

Z

Straightforward Strategies and Tactics for Business Today

The **Que Biz-Tech series** is designed for the legions of executives and marketers out there trying to come to grips with emerging technologies that can make or break their business. These books help the reader know what's important, what isn't, and provide deep inside know-how for entering the brave new world of business technology, covering topics such as mobile marketing, microblogging, and iPhone and iPad app marketing.

- Straightforward strategies and tactics for companies who are either using or will be using a new technology/product or way of thinking/ doing business

- Written by well known industry experts in their respective fields— and designed to be an open platform for the author to teach a topic in the way he or she believes the audience will learn best

- Covers new technologies that companies must embrace to remain competitive in the marketplace and shows them how to maximize those technologies for profit

- Written with the marketing and business user in mind—these books meld solid technical know-how with corporate-savvy advice for improving the bottom line

Visit **quepublishing.com/biztech** to learn more about the **Que Biz-Tech series**

FREE Online Edition

Your purchase of **Smart Business, Social Business** includes access to a free online edition for 45 days through the Safari Books Online subscription service. Nearly every Que book is available online through Safari Books Online, along with more than 5,000 other technical books and videos from publishers such as Addison-Wesley Professional, Cisco Press, Exam Cram, IBM Press, O'Reilly, Prentice Hall, and Sams.

SAFARI BOOKS ONLINE allows you to search for a specific answer, cut and paste code, download chapters, and stay current with emerging technologies.

Activate your FREE Online Edition at
www.informit.com/safarifree

> **STEP 1:** Enter the coupon code: RUARWBI.

> **STEP 2:** New Safari users, complete the brief registration form.
>   Safari subscribers, just log in.

Addison Wesley · Adobe Press · ALPHA · Cisco Press · FT Press · IBM Press · lynda.com · Microsoft Press · New Riders

O'REILLY · Peachpit Press · PRENTICE HALL · QUE · Redbooks · SAMS · SAS · Sun · WILEY